Roy & Irv

Conversations

1

Doug Rucker

Roy & Irv
Conversations - 1

By Doug Rucker
Layout by Helane Freeman

Doug Rucker
Vilimapubco
Malibu, California
ruckerdoug@gmail.com

For permission requests, sales to U.S. bookstores and
wholesalers, or to inquire about quantity discounts,
please contact the publisher at the email address above.

Library of Congress Control Number: 2024925892

ISBN – 978-1-7354717-6-1

First Edition
10 9 8 7 6 5 4 3 2 1

Printed in the United States of America

Roy & Irv

Conversations

1

Contents

Forward

The idea for Roy & Irv was inspired by a comedy book I'd written in 2017 called *A Book About Everyday Stuff with Jorge and Merle.* Jorge and Merle were talking dogs with a close personal relationship. Jorge was older, could write poetry and was intellectually astute. Merle, with the energy of an adolescent boy, played with Jorge as his companion. With interesting conversations about the activities of one or the other they discussed poetry, humor, philosophies and psychologies.

Being an architect, writer and artist, the author's Dharma at 93-years-old had already arrived. After reading almost a thousand books in 20-years, I felt I knew a lot, but had run out of things to build, draw or say. According to my three daughters, I seemed tired and more submissive toward life - in other words, ready to die. Late-age ankle infections led to developing Edema in both legs. They'd swollen in size that forced me into compact stockings and urination pills hoping to increase the quality of my tired blood. Through the affects of compact stockings, urination pills and reading a very special book by Stephen Cope about Dharma called *The Great Work of Your Life,* I began to return to my more reasonable life.

Stephen's book is on finding the main work of your life. I had already done four of my Dharma's in athletics, architecture, writing and art. At my advanced age I decided I'd like to write something by just letting it fall out of my head – hopefully to which there would be no end. I asked myself what was that? I used experience I already had, like automatic writing and analyzing 50 of my dreams, understanding 154 of my own *Abstract Drawings,* and studying the meaning of 66 *No Think* photographs. They added to my insight. Extensive writing of over 30 books added more to an already active mind.

No Think Drawings, Dreams and Abstract Artwork are representative of one of the two parts of the human brain of which are called *Feeling* and *Reasoning.* They also could be termed the *Conscious, (Reasoning)* and *Unconscious (Feeling).* The book of Roy and Irv are representative of both *Conscious* and *Unconscious* portions of the brain. The following is a look inside my brain at the *unconscious.* Let's see who I am.

Mayfly

Irv – Hallo Roy!

Roy – It's been a long time. How long's it ben?

Irv – Ah'd say 15 minutes.

Roy – Dat's not long.

Irv – It is fo' a *Mayfly*.

Roy – Well, ah'm not no *Mayfly*.

Irv – Well wat kind o' fly are yu?

Roy – Ah'm ain' no fly at all. Ah'm a person an' always will be a person. Yu sure ar' dumb!

Irv – Ah kno' *Mayflies* only live 24 hours. But, did yu kno' fo' a *Mayfly*, birth to deth takes a year?

Roy – Whose?

Irv – *Mayflies!* Who's da dumb one now?

Roy - Dat reminds me o' taxes.

Irv – Wy?

Roy – They neber give me enough time to pay.

    Irv – Yu're nev'r given a year to pay yore taxes! Yu sure ar' dumb!

Roy – Ah gess we're both dumb. Let's hab a dumb contest. Ah bet yu win!

    Irv – OK! Ask me a quest-shun.

Roy – Whose smarter a bird or a fish?

    Irv – Dat's a dumb question.

Roy – Wy doan yu tink o' a smart quest-shun?

    Irv – How about somethin' lak, Wa's an *illusion?*

Roy – Heck! Dat's an easy one. An *illusion* is somethin' way differnt fum *reality.*

    Irv – Wa's *reality?*

Roy – Ah'm a da one askin' da quest-shuns! Yu're supposed to kno' wat *reality is?*

    Irv - Sometimes Ah do an' sometimes ah doan.

Roy – Dis is a contest o' who is da dumbest.

Irv – Ah'm giving it all ah got.

Roy – Well, it ain' much.

Irv – If, *reality* wa different, wud dat make yur hair stand on end?

Roy – Yu mean if it wud be scary?

Irv – Yeah! Ma hair wud stan straight up an' da sight o' it wud blow yur mind dat wud suddenly run *tepid*.

Roy – How yu kno' all dis?

Irv – *Intuition!*

Roy – Wa's *Intuition?*

Irv – Ah look in ma brain an' up pops da answer.

Roy – No thought at all?

Irv – Ah doan need no thought! Thought's jus' lookin' fo' trouble.

Roy – We're not getting anywer' wif our quest fo' da ultimate dumbness. Wy doan yu ask me sumthin else?

Irv – How high is up?

Roy – Infinitely high. Eberyone kno's dat. Das a dumb question. Yu hab jus' won de prize by askin' de dumbest question in da contest.

Irv – Lots o' people doan kno' da sky is *infinitely* high.

Roy – Heck! Ah kno' it!

Irv - Ma uncle *Hardie* doesn' kno' da sky includes all o' outer space.

Roy – Yeah! But yu cain't see all o' outer space, especially dat portion including 2.73-Kelvin temperature thru wich flows light at 186 thousand miles a second.

Irv – Heck! Ah knew dat!

Metaphors and Stuff

2

Roy – Hay Irv, wa'er yoo doin' wif yore life?

Irv – Nuthin.

Roy – Dat's wa ah thoat. Now's da time to start doin' sumthin special.

Irv – Ah'm tinkin o' taken up bein' a famus *psychiatrist-bunky*.

Roy – Yu mean *psychiatrist* wif no *"bunky"* on de end.

Irv – Heck! Ah knew dat! Ah wa jus' pullin' yur leg.

Roy – Well, try pullin' a fast one, instead.

Irv – Lak, *"Wait 'til de sun shines Nelli"*

Roy – Ah doan kno' nobody named *Nelli*!

Irv - Dat's sort o' a *metaphor*.

Roy – Wa's a *met-a-fo'*?

Irv – A *met-a-fo'* is not *"fo'"* anything. Who's da dumb one now?

Roy – Ah thoat da phrase, "*Dat party wa a bomb!*" wa a *metaphor.*

   Irv - How-ju get dat?

Roy – Frum de *Internet!*

   Irv – Yoo-ure so dumb, yu got to use da *Internet?*

Roy – No! Ah'm so smart, ah use da *Internet.*

   Irv – Heck! Ah neva use da *Internet.*

Roy – Dat's wy yoo-ure so dumb.

   Irv – How about "*Ding-Dong, Da Bells is Goin' to Chime!*"

Roy – Wa's dat mean? Yu are a *Ding-Dong* an' yu ar' goin' to let loose wif somethin' da worl' hab neva herd o' before?

   Irv – Yeah! Yu got it! How bout da clouds hab a *personality?*

Roy – Yeah! Look up in de sky an' wat do yu see?

   Irv – Ah see da ceiling. We're inside. Heck! Ah knew dat.

Roy – If we were outside yude see *fair weddr* clouds. Dey'd be wite, o' course.

Irv – Heck! Ah kno' clouds are wite.

Roy – Sometimes dey'r gray.

Irv - Not fair-weddr clouds.

Roy – We're goin' to get into an argument bout wheddr da clouds outside ar' wite or gray?

Irv – Well, jus' look an' see!

Roy – OK! Ah jus' looked tru de window. Dey'r wite. Wat personality do dey hab?

Irv – *Dey'r a little peek-ed cause der modder dint approve o' woo dey were datin'.*

Roy – Do clouds hab dates?

Irv – Only a few o' em. Only da ones dat hab *fathers*.

Roy – Wa about da ones dat doan hab no *fathers?*

Irv – De ones dat doan hab no *fathers* ar' not yet born.

Roy – Ah can see dat. But yooo're missing da *point.*

Irv – Wa da *point?*

Roy – De point is yu doan unnerstan' da *point*.

   Irv – De *point* is yu doan unnerstan da *answer*.

Roy – Der is no *answer*.

   Irv – How about *La-La-La Hoop-de-Do or Dingle-Berry-Doo-Doo-Doo?*

Roy – Tha's ridiculous. Wy cain't we end dis conversation wif somethin' brilliant to teach readers, some faint, but important truth dey may neber hab herd before?

   Irv – Ah thoaght de *Personality o' Clouds* covered dat'.

Meat Choppin'

3

Roy – Watcha got to say, Irv?

Irv – Not much, Roy.

Roy - Haben't yu got some tales to make ma *blood run cole?*

Irv – Ah broke ma *manicured* nail dis mornin'.

Roy – Since wen yu *manicure* yer nails?

Irv - Since ah wen to ma sister's prom las' nite.

Roy – Who'd ja go wif?

Irv – Nobo-died yu kno'. Her name's, *Harriet.* She is really good lookin' in her long, wite gown.

Roy – Ah'd lak to meet her.

Irv – She's *nine-feet-six tall.*

Roy - Dat's big. How tall ar' yu?

Irv – *Five-foot-six.*

Roy – Yu're quite a *Mismatch.*

  Irv – She's also a *Millionaire.*

Roy – Has she got a *Girl-fren'?*

  Irv – Yeah! *Ida!*

Roy – How tall is she?

  Irv – *Three-foot-six?*

Roy – Dey'r quite a *Mismatch.*

  Irv – She's also a *Millionaire.*

Roy – Dey'r financially *Matched.*

  Irv – We're broken up.

Roy – Wy's dat?

  Irv – In dis expensive house wif a hunderd so guests, while kissing her stomach, ah pushed her too hard 'gainst a broken railin' an' she fell one story upside down an' splashed into a swimmmin' pool.

Roy – Dat's embarrassin'.

  Irv – Dancing next to us, *Ida* also fell an' did a

couple o' flip-flops head over heels into da pool.

Roy – Wa anyone hurt?

Irv - They were OK, but embarrassed an' soakin' wet. Took der *Rolls Royce's* home.

Roy – How de yu get home?

Irv – *Streetcar!*

Roy – So, watcha goin' to do now?

Irv – Ah'm gonna' *wait right here til de sun doan shine.*

Roy – Eben if it's for-eber?

Irv – Ah'm gonna' *wait right here, wait right here, wait right here, til de sun doan shine.*

Roy - Isn' dat some kinda song?

Irv – Yep! Ah took up singin' right after her fall into da pool.

Roy - Habin any success wif it?

Irv – Ma neighbor offered me *$20.00* to quit.

Roy – Dat's a success. Got any other jobs?

  Irv – Gotta' job at de meat market.

Roy – How much yu makin' der?

  Irv – Forty bucks an' all de *cow-leg* ah can keep down.

Roy –Kno-in yu, dat's a pretty gud deal. Yu goin' fo' broke on da *cow-leg* job?

  Irv – Ah'd rather be singin'.

Roy – Cain't yooo do *both*?

  Irv – Sing while ah'm chompin' down a cow-leg?

Roy – Yu could do *"Ah'm a Yankee Doodle Dandy. Yankee Doodle do or Die. A real live nephew o' ma Uncle Sam, born on de fourth o' July."* Yu culd make a big success in da *Unidy States*.

  Irv – Ah aint no George M. Cohan!

Needle in Haystack 4

Irv – Hey! Roy. Ah got a *quest-shun* fo' ya.

Roy – Ah just love *quest-shun's*.

Irv – Yu always claim yu kno' *eber-thing*.

Roy – Ah try to stay modest fo' ma audience.

Irv – How big is da *Earth?*

Roy – Bigger dan de *Moooon*.

Irv – Heck! Ah knew dat! Ah mean, how much do da *world weigh!*

Roy – Twenty-five pounds.

Irv – Ah'm tryin' to be serious, an' yore makin' a joke.

Roy – Yore question's ain' smart.

Irv – Ah tink ahm askin' da wrong person.

Roy – Off hand, ah doan kno' how big da *Earth* is. Ask a *scientist*.

Irv – Ah doan kno' no *scientists*.

Roy – Less see in da *Internet* – de radius is 3,958-miles, an da diameter is 7,926-miles an' da circumference is 24,901-miles.

Irv – *Ma Gumball!* How ju do dat?

Roy – Jus' checkin' da *Internet*.

Irv – Ah doan hab no *Internet*.

Roy – If yu hab an *Internet* yu can exchange it fo' brains.

Irv – Ah've already got brains.

Roy – Ah haben't seen any.

Irv – Ah found brains last *Saturday*. Yu've got to *search* an' *search* an' *searching search*.

Roy – Yeah? Wa did yu search fo'?

Irv – *A Needle in de Haystack*.

Roy – Yu searched fo' *A Needle in de Haystack?* Ah doan believe yu'd be capable o' dat'.

Irv – No! Ah found it an' hid it again to test yu, in case yu din't kno' how big da worl' wa.

Roy - Heck! Ah could find dat in a minute. *Wer's de Haystack?*

Irv - It's right outside on da vacant lot!

Roy - Ah gotta see dis. *(Goes outside.)* Well! Sure enough! Der's da *Haystack*. Wer's da *Needle?*

Irv - Dat's fo' yu to fine'.

Roy - Heck! Ah can see it frum here!

Irv - Yu can? Ah doan see it.

Roy - Yu also hid it fum yo-sef.

Irv - Yu wer' supposed to find it an' yu did.

Roy - Dat attests to ma superior brains.

Irv - Yeah! Well wa da interior o' da earth made o'?

Roy - Check yo *Internet!* Mostly iron and nickel wif itsy bitsy amounts o' gold, cobalt an' platnum.

Irv - Using de *Internet* fo' brains, ah see!

Roy - Ah've got ma own brain!

Irv - Ah've not seen any.

Roy – Copycat!

    Irv – Fo' eber-lastin goodness on da face o' da *Earth*, ah call fo' da power o' life to overcome all disasters an' provide an ultimate heben on *Earth*.

Roy – Wa does dat mean?

    Irv – Ah understand wat yu mean, but cain't go 'long wif it cause ah doan feel ma *interior pull*.

Roy – Perhaps yu'd feel da *interior pull* if yu gave yur-self a yank. Da effort to move sump-times encourages de attempt.

    Irv – Yu should kno'.

Crazy Grass 5

Roy – Ah'm going to reveal something so fantastic, yu'll wet yur pants.

Irv – Blessed are yu! Ah cain't wait to wet ma pants! Ah jus' changed *unner-wear*, too.

Roy – Water makes de grass grow *wild!*

Irv – Ah'm *drownin'* in ma own urine. Dats common kno'ledge. Ah could hab tole yu dat.

Roy – But it's da *"wild"* part dats so *meanin-ful.*

Irv – Wy is *"wild"* so important?

Roy – *"Wild"* means out o' control, deranged, crackers, barking mad.

Irv – How could *grass* go *barking mad.*

Roy – When it's lost its sense o' being. When it no longer kno's who it is. When it's part *Uni-berse* an' part dream. When it feels it's neither here nor der.

Irv – Ah tink ah understand wa yu hab to say bout *"wild"* grass, tho ah doan suspect dat grass tinks.

Roy – Dwell on falseness too much an' it becums real!

  Irv – Are yu playing wif ma mind?

Roy – Maybe a little bit.

  Irv – Do yu really believe wat yu said bout *"wild"* glass? Ah mean *"wild"* grass?

Roy – *"Wild"* grass isn't as crazy as yu wud tink.

  Irv – It's not?

Roy – Consider da extinkt dinosaur *Tyrannosaurus Rex*, King o' da tyrant lizards. It's one o' da best represented *Therapods*.

  Irv – Ib *Tyrannosaurus Rex* frightening?

Roy – Wif horrendous teeth an' tiny arms it scattered fear among other dinosaurs such as de *Triceratops, Ankylosaurus* an' *Edmontosaurus*.

  Irv - Yu're pullin' ma leg. Wher'd ju get dat infomation?

Roy – De *computer*.

  Irv - Maybe ah'll get a *computer*.

Roy – If yu tink grass is *"wild"*, just consider *Tyrannosaurus Rex*.

Irv – How bout ah consid'r ma *Modd-er-in-law?*

Roy – Is she scary?

Irv – Teenager's came over at *Holloween* an' she wacked em wif a butcher knife.

Roy – Ah warn't tinkin bout domestic stuff. More natural stuff lak *grass* an' *dinosaurs.*

Irv – But *grass* ain' goin' no-wer an' *dinosaurs* ar' dead. Ah'm not scar'd o' dem'.

Roy – Wa scares yu?

Irv – Takin' de *streetcar?*

Roy – Der ain' no *streetcars* anymore.

Irv – OK! Ah used to be scared o' takin' da *street-car* eben tho it isn't der anymore.

Roy – Forget wat used to scare yu. We ain' livin' in no past. Wa scares yu now?

Irv – Parachutin' out o' an *aero-plane.*

Roy – Most people are 'fraid o' dat'.

Irv – Yu sure ar' hard to please. How 'bout crossin' da double line an' bein' smacked by a speedin' truck?

Roy – Heck! *Eberybody's* 'fraid o' dat! Cain't yu give me sumthin more excitin' dan dat, dis essay's almos' ober.

Irv – How *'bout de world blowin'* up, or, da *Uni-berse* runnin' out o' gas. Or *de ocean over-flowin'?*

Roy – Dat could happen.

Mono-Monster

6

Roy – Are we gettin' into it?

Irv – Gettin' into wat?

Roy – Wa-eber we talkin' 'bout?

Irv – Lets talk about fishin'.

Roy – Wa kindo fishin'?

Irv - Catchin' *bigguns*.

Roy – Yu eber catch *bigguns?*

Irv – Ah caught a *Fishy-Eyed Mono-Monster* once.

Roy – Ah neber heard o' a *Fishy-Eyed Mono-Monster*.

Irv – It's de biggest fish in *Lake Michigan*. Lives in da dark bottom o' da lake an' has fourteen octopuses fo' breakfast.

Roy – How big is dis *Fishy-Eyed Wa- yu-call-it?*

Irv – As big as a *yatch*.

Roy – How big is a *yatch?*

Irv – Forty-feet plus.

Roy – Wa dja use fo' bate?

Irv – *Uncle Henry.*

Roy – Dat's murder.

Irv – We didn' purposely use em fo' bate. He got caught in fishin' lines an' wa pulled 50-feet in da air screamin' lak a *banshee.*

Roy - Wa's a *banshee?*

Irv – A female spirit in *Gaelic Folklore* whose wailin' warns dat death will soon occur in de *Neighborhood.*

Roy – Wa do it soun' lak'?

Irv – Now yu soun' lak de *dumb* one.

Roy – Ah repeat wat do it soun' lak?

Irv – It soun' lak screamin', wailin', shriekin' an' keenin'.

Roy – Wa's *keenin'?*

Irv – A long, loud, sad soun' fo' someone who has died. How come ah kno' more dan yu?

Roy – Nobody's *perfect.*

Irv - Especially yu!

Roy – Did Uncle Henry escape deth?

Irv – Yeah! He's here, but stayin' too long in de can.

Roy – How did yu land de *Fishy-Eyed Mono-Monster?*

Irv - He landed us! While we were in de boat he whipped us up 30-feet in da air til da line broke an' we sailed by da wind a hunderd-feet before we smashed into de lake an' wa dumped outa de boat into icy lake water.

Roy – Wow! Dat wa really an adventure. Yu wanna go *fishin'* again?

Irv - Ah tink ah've had it fo' *fishin'.*

Roy – So? Wa-cha wanna do now?

Irv - Ah tink ah'm gonna knit ma-sef another hat.

Roy – Yu knit hats?

Irv - Just a little now an' den - fo' ma-sef.

Roy – How many hats yu got?

Irv – Ah hab over five-hundred an' forty-seben hats, all o' differnt colors an' styles stored in de shed wif walls, but no roof.

Roy – Do yu eber *wear* dem?

Irv – Ah *wear* differnt ones ebery holiday.

Roy - Wa one are yu *wearing* fo' *Christmas?*

Irv – Ah'm wearin' ma Santa Claus hat wif bells hanging down ober ma ears dat play *Silent Night* an' *Jingle Bells* til yore ready to scream.

Roy – Dat's Chrismassy!

Irv – It's better dan being tossed in de air by a *Fishy-Eyed Mono-Monster.*

Maccu Pichu

7

Roy – Hey Irv! Der's sumthin urgent ah've got to tell yu. It's not about yur *brother or sister* o' any o' yur famibly.

Irv – Ah doan hab no *brother or sister*, an' ma folks is vacationin' in *Washinton State*.

Roy – Ah registered yu in de U. S. Lottery fo' $2 an' yu won a thousan' dollars an' a trip to *Maccu Piccu, Peru*.

Irv – Wow! Yu did? An' ah doan eben speak *Spanish*, or wa-eber der language is. When do ah leab?

Roy – Yu're supposed to leab *Saturday* on da 23rd o' *October*.

Irv – Let me check ma schedule, ah'm meetin' *Fred* fo' ice cream on de 22nd an' *Sally* on de 23rd. She's goin' to tell me 'bout her boyfriend. Can ah postpone de trip?

Roy – Ah doan tink so, da boat is leabin on da 23rd.

Irv – Cain't ah take da plane?

Roy - We can call de *Lottery* an' ah'll fine out. Ah'll do it now. *(Hangs up and Ring! Ring! Ring!)* Hello, *Lottery?* Dis is Roy callin' 'bout Irv's trip to *Machi Piccu, Peru.*

Lottery - Yeah? Wa daya want?

Roy - Irv won a trip to *Maccu Pichu, Peru* an' can he take da plane to *Peru?*

Lottery - Nah! We doan give no fake airplane rides.

Roy - Can' yu give us da money yu would hab spent on da trip fo' de plane ticket?

Lottery - Yu tink we're some kinda *Sander Clause?* O' course not!

Roy - *(Calls Irv.)* De answer is *No!*

Irv - OK! Ah'll call Sally an' tell her ah cain't make it!

Roy - Better *Maccu Pichu* than a date wif Sally!

Irv - Hello Sally? Ah've got to cancel fo' de 23rd o' October.

Sally - Yu mean *September!*

Irv - Yu mean ah got our dates wrong?

Sally – Looks lak it, *Dipshit!*

Irv – *Dipshit?* Yu're callin' me a *Dipshit?*

Sally – Dis is de fourth time yu've missed our date an' ah aina gonna stan' fo' it no mo'!

Irv – Well, ah'm sorreee! *(Hangs up!)*

Roy – Well, wa'd ja fine out?

Irv – She's no longer talkin' to me an' called me a *Dipshit!*

Roy – Yu kno', she's partially rite. At times yu can be a *Dipshit.*

Irv – Ah got some faults, but ah doan tink ah'm no *Dipshit!*

Roy – *Dipshit! Dipshit!* Der goes da *Dipshit!*

Irv – Yu doan hab to make no song out o' it.

Roy – *Dipshit* or not, we can go bowlin'. Ah've got a free hour comin' at *Bowl-a-Bunk* in *Chatsworth.*

Irv – Dat's great, Roy. Ah could use a little *bowl-a-bunkin'* in ma life. *Bowl-a-bunk, Bowl-a-bunk,* wone yu be ma *Bowl-a-bunk?*

Roy – It's not a song, yu kno'.

Irv - Sweet *Bowl-a-bunk*, ma *Bowl-a-bunk*, at night, *Sweetheart*, fo' yu ah *Bowl-a-bunk* – an' stunk.

Roy – It's yu dat stinks. We should be drinking.

Irv - Ah want to get stinkin' drunk!

Roy – Yu're already stinkin'. Here's a scotch an' soda.

Irv – Jus' wa ah need. Gulp! Gulp! Gulp!

Roy – Sure doan take yu long to get *stupefied*.

Irv – Ah started wen ah wa a kid.

Guah! Guah! Guah! 8

Irv – How ya doin' Roy? Goin' down fo' lunch?

Roy – Naw! Got a toothache?

Irv – Which one?

Roy – De upjaw, sidewise, *molar-bunky*.

Irv – Let me see! Wow! Yur face is swollen to de size o' a large pumpkin dat rolling down a hill could derail a truck dat smackin' a storefront could send bananas all ova de street.

Roy – It doan look dat bad!

Irv - Yes! It do! It swelled up an' look lak it goin' to explode an' take off yur whole haid leabin a bloody neck-stump to make us all trow up.

Roy – No it doan! Yu makin' a mountain out o' a *beetle-hill*.

Irv – Hab it yur own way. Wa'-cha gonna do now?

Roy – Goin' to de denist!

   Irv – Das smart!

Roy – O' course it's smart. Das wer ah'm goin'. Yu cumin wif me?

   Irv – Ah wa goin' to see a man 'bout a *pet lizard*.

Roy - Forget de *pet lizard*. Cum wif me.

   Irv – Sho is a nice day.

Roy – Ah'm in pain an' yu're talkin' 'bout de good day?

   Irv – It's nice out.

Roy – Cain't yu tink o' sumtin else, lak de time yu lost yore brakes an' smacked da pole?

   Irv - Tha's too unhappy. Ah could tell yu 'bout ma new *girl-fren'*.

Roy – OK!

   Irv – She went roller-skatin', fell down an' *boomped* her haid.

Roy – Wa she *boomp* it on?

   Irv - *Cement.*

Roy - She OK?

Irv - Yeah! She got a shot.

Roy - Ah din't tink dey giv shots to ladies who *boomped* der head.

Irv - Only if der eyes are whirlin' roun an' dey forget who dey ar'.

Roy - Soun' lak she shud be in de horse-spital.

Irv - De Doktor say de shot wud take care o' it.

Roy - Ah hope she do dat. We at de dentist's office now, an' goin' in.

Irv - Nice place yu got here, Doc.

Roy - Dis is *Nebula*, ma dentist. *Nebula*, dis is Irv.

Nebula - Howja do, Irv. Roy, cum dis way an' sit right down here facin' de window wif da two-story brick buildings outside wif no windlows starin' yu in da face.

Roy - Thanks, Bob. May ah call yu by yore first name, Bob?

Nebula - Yu doan need to be formal roun here. Lemmee see dat tooth. Whooo! Das' a good one. Rubbin' ma hans, ah'm sure goin' to hab fun on dis one.

Roy – Hope it's not too bad.

Nebula – De tougher dey are, de more money ah make. Yu sure yu got enuff money to pay fo' *Dis Doozey?*

Roy – If it's pain or loss o' money, ah'm kickin' in wif de big bucks.

Nebula – Das wat yu should be doin'. Bzzzzzzzzz!

Roy – *Guah! Guah! Guah!*

Irv – Yu OK, Roy?

Roy - *Guah! Guah! Guah!*

Irv – Yu sure hab to hand it to ol' Roy. He takes pain wer' he finds it an' deals wif it.

Roy – *Guah! Guah! Guah!*

Brake Job

9

Roy – Hey, Irv, ah hear yu got a *brake* job.

Irv - Yeah! De ol' *brakes* went bloowy on me while ah wa coastin' down *Kill-yur-self Hill*.

Roy – Das one tough hill to lose yur *brakes* on. Obviously da hill dint fulfill its prophecy.

Irv - Ah swerved to da left, missed a big rock, slammed between two oak trees, hit a rock, den bounced down da hill to wind up straddlin a ragin' creek.

Roy – Were ya hurt?

Irv - Ah got a scratch on ma big toe. Ah called de toe-truck service an' *Joe* pulled me out.

Roy – Wanna get a sandwich?

Irv – One o' doe's big ones at *Giantburger?*

Roy – Sure! They sell enormous burgers. Wa's da biggest burger yu eber ate?

Irv – Ah tried to get down a 25-pound burger, but tossed ma cookies at 13.5 pounds.

Roy – Lost da bet, ay?

   Irv – Ah came in 2nd.

Roy – How many pounds did da winner keep down?

   Irv – Ah wooo-nt say *"keep down"* ar' de right words. He later barfed it into kingdom cum.

Roy – Ah'm always amazed at life's *re-speriences*. Remines me o' de time ah wa hit by a train.

   Irv – A train hit yu?

Roy – Ah wa almos' hit by a train. Ah wa walkin' down de tracks, mindin' ma own business, wonderin' how ah wa goin' to keep da tomatoes alive afta de big freeze.

   Irv – Den wa hoppen?

Roy – De train cum likidy speedin' down de track, whistle blowin' – *which ah din hear* – an' whipped off ma T-shirt til ah wa naked as a jaybird frm da belt up, an' lyin' on da groun' wif da train hustle-bustlin' faster dan a jaybird chased by a skunk.

   Irv – *Wowy-Dowy!* Dat soun' mighty precarious. Wa ju' do den?

Roy – After de train wen by, ah got up, wipped de dust off ma pants, looked fo' ma T-shirt, put it on, an' walked home.

Irv – Boy! Das really sump-fin. Makes me wanna sing.

Roy – Das strange. Wa fo' yu wanna sing?

Irv – Cause ahm ticklin' ma-sef. Ha! Ha! Ha!

Roy – Irv, cum back an' go normal!

Irv – Isn' singin' normal?

Roy – Only fo' *Louis Armstrong.*

Irv – Yu kno' *Louis?*

Roy – Ah doan kno' him. Ah met him once.

Irv – Wha did he say?

Roy – How de do! Ah doan kno' wa he said. He wa polite!

Irv – Did ol' Satchmo introduce yu to *Ella Fitzgerald,* or sing yu *Mack de Knife?*

Roy – Nope!

Irv – Wa did he do?

Roy – He shook hans wif eber-buddy an' walked out de do.

Irv - Do yu feel yur life has changed?

Roy – Nope!

Irv - Is *"Nope"* all yu got to say?

Roy – Nope.

Barefoot in de Park 10

Roy – Wa different Irv?

Irv – *Thoat!*

Roy – Yeah! Yu're right! Who tinks, anymore?

Irv – Not me.

Roy – Das no surprise.

Irv – How 'bout yu? Did yu eber gib thoat to any-ting?

Roy - A long time ago.

Irv – Wa wa it 'bout?

Roy – Goin' to de movies.

Irv – Wa ja see?

Roy – *Barefoot in de Park.* Ah wanda kno' wy dey wa *barefoot.*

Irv - Dey wer'nt *barefoot.* Yu could see da 'hole movie an' no-wer wer dey *barefoot.*

Roy – Yu seen da '*hole movie?*

 Irv – Yeah! Ah seen da '*hole movie.*

Roy – Wa year wa da *movie* made?

 Irv – 1967?

Roy - How ol' are yu?

 Irv – Ah'm 41.

Roy – Wa year is now?

 Irv – 2025! Anybody kno's dat.

Roy – 1967 is 58 years ago. Yu ain' dat old.

 Irv – Ah didn' see it until 2008 when ah wa 25.

Roy – Yu lie!

 Irv – Ah ain' no lier.

Roy – Yu lie through yore *teeth!*

 Irv – Ah doan hab no *teeth.*

Roy – Yu lyin' right now. Ah kin see yore *teeth.*

 Irv – OK! Sometimes ah lie, but dis one '*bout* da movie ain' one o' dem.

Roy – OK! Ah believe yu now. But fo' a while, yu had me *Ding-Donged.*

Irv – Ah wud nevr tell yu no lies, but yur feet are too big!

Roy – No dey not!

Irv – How big are dey'?

Roy – Size 14.

Irv – Das way too big.

Roy – How big are yore feet?

Irv – A pretty 7-1/2.

Roy – Das too small. At least ah cud go happily *Barefoot in de Park.*

Irv – Ah already tole yu, dey didn' go happily *Barefoot in de Park.*

Roy – Den, wy dey name de *picty-ure* dat way?

Irv – To make money.

Roy – Do yu want money?

Irv – Eberybody do!

Roy – Whadaya wanna make money at?

   Irv – Sumthin' original dat eberybody lak's.

Roy – Lak, wa dat?

   Irv – Ah always thoat o' dancin' on a twig.

Roy – Thas imaginative, but ah doan kno' if da idea wud sell.

   Irv – Ah'll call de salesman – or sales lady, because ah need women in ma life.

Roy – Ah can visualize it now. Hey lady, ah wan' yu to sell de idea o' dancin' on twig.

   Irv – No! Das not it.

Roy – Den, shee say, Das de stupides' idee-a ah eber herd in ma life!

   Irv – No! It's not.

Roy – De lady say, *"Ah got to cross de park to catch a bus."*

   Irv – At least she's not *Barefoot in de Park.*

Madagascar 11

Roy – Well, it's a day later. Wa-aya got to say?

Irv Life's a kick.

Roy – Somebody kick yu?

Irv –No! Life's not ded.

Roy – Yu doan kno' wa life is?

Irv –Ah kno' wa life isn't.

Roy – Heck! Eben ah kno' wa life isn't. Anybody can tell yu wa life isn't.

Irv –Yeah? Wa isn't life?

Roy – Any-ting not alive.

Irv –Yeah? Wa dat?

Roy – A rock, das wat.

Irv –Yu cheated.

Roy – Ah did not. OK! Wa isn't life?

Irv – Ah already tole yu. Any-ting das *dead*.

Roy – OK! Wa's true?

Irv – Any-ting dats not false.

Roy – Now we're talkin' *opposites*. Up is not down. In is not out. Ober is not under.

Irv – Heck! Ah could hab tol yu dat.

Roy – Yeah! But yu din't.

Irv – Yu din't ask me.

Roy – OK! Wa $E=mc^2$?

Irv – Heck! Ah doan kno'.

Roy – See? Ah tole yu, yu're dumb!

Irv – Yeah! Here's one fo' yu! How many stars in de' *Uni-berse?*

Roy – Well over 100!

Irv – Yu're right. OK! Yu're smarter dan me.

Roy – Ah'm sorry 'bout dat, but facks ar' facks.

Irv – If 14 sausages make a baloney, how many sausages make a thousan' baloneys?

Roy – Enough to las' yu to get to *Madagascar.*

Irv – By God, yu're right! Ah've got to hand it to yu. Ah hereby relinquish ma smart-title to Roy, *King o' de Downtrodden.*

Roy – Ah ain' no *King o' de Downtrodden.* Ah'm *King o' de Uptrodden.*

Irv – Wa dat?

Roy – Back to *opposites again.* Doan yu kno' da differnce between *Up an' Down.* Anybody kno's it. Ah kno's it.

Irv – Wer's *Madagascar?*

Roy – An island off da Southeast Coast o' *Africa.*

Irv – Is it a rich cuntry?

Roy – No! It's poverty-stricken an' subjeck to political unrest, though it has sum fine lookin' *Ring-tailed Lemurs.*

Irv – Yu want to go der?

Roy – If ah rode in an *iron-enclosed* car.

Irv – Yu'd be safe frum bombin'.

Roy – Dats de idea.

Irv –Hey! Less *NOT* go to *Madagascar* fo' a vacation.

Roy – Finally we hab somthin' to agree on. We both doan wan' to go to no *Madagascar*.

Irv – Wer else cud we go?

Roy – *Mars* is dry, but cold. Yu wanna go der?

Irv –It wud take 9-months o' *rocket-trabel*. On de way we could play *Scrabble*.

Roy – Ah doan tink ah cud take dat much time playin' *Scrabble*.

Irv –Just tink o' *Mars* atmosphere.

Roy – Or lack therof.

Estigast 12

Roy – How ole are yu, Irv?

  Irv – Ole enough to kno' better. *Yuck! Yuck! Yuck!*

Roy – No, seriously?

  Irv - Ah'm 41, goin' on 42.

Roy – Wa else would yu be goin' on?

  Irv – 43!

Roy – Cain't yu be serious fo' a moment?

  Irv – When ah'm serious ah get *criti-cizm.*

Roy – See? Das no answer!

  Irv – Yur reply wa a *criti-cizm.*

Roy – Doan hang me!

  Irv – Yurself mus be criticized.

Roy – Ah do not need to be *criti-cizm.*

  Irv – Yu argue all da time.

Roy – Wa yu tink 'bout global warmin'?

  Irv - Ah tink it sucks.

Roy – Wa else sucks?

  Irv – Sometimes yore attitude.

Roy – Screw yu!

  Irv - Screw yu, too!

Roy – *Ego Feego, Feder-ego.*

  Irv – *Sock-it-me, Samoa-Tree, fo' Listnen to Yore Poe-Tree.*

Roy – *One fo' de Money, Two fo' de Show, Tree to get Redy an' Four to Trow Up Yur Flabber-Estigast.*

  Irv – Wa's *Flabber-Estigast?*

Roy – An *Estigast* dat's Flabby.

  Irv – Wa's an *Estigast?*

Roy – An *Estigast* is a small animal ah just invented dat catches its tail in its mouth wif a fast whirl.

Irv – Wa do it look lak?

Roy – Lak a *de-mented Meercat*.

Irv – Will it eat me?

Roy – Only wen yu pull its tail.

Irv – Ah'ma not a goin' to do dat!

Roy - Yu doan talk good!

Irv – Yu ain' so good yur-self.

Roy – OK! Ah'm sorry. Wa else is goin' on?

Irv – In ma mind, ah jus got bak frum da dark side o' da moon!

Roy – How's it der'?

Irv – It's nite-time all de time.

Roy – Any good lookin' stars?

Irv – Der's a *plethora* o' good lookin' stars.

Roy – Wa does *plethora* mean?

Irv – *Excessive quantity or profusion.*

Roy – Just lak yore brains.

Irv – Not dat ah see.

Roy – Cuase ah tink ah'm so great?

Irv - Ah just see ego!

Roy – Wa does de darkened side o' de moon look lak?

Irv – As yu wud *Xpect*, it looks kinda lak da a shaded visible side.

Roy – Any other memorable *experiences?*

Irv – There is one important moment fo' me ah *experienced* wile on da dark side o' da moon.

Roy – Wa dat?

Irv – Ah entered 2.73-degrees-Kelvin o' empty space encompassing billions o' galaxies dat each contained a black hole. Ah wa lost in reberie fo' five-minutes frum ma own simple world.

Roy – Irving, sometimes *yu're a poet an' doan noet'.*

Hoboken 13

Roy – Whadaya goin' to do today, Irv?

Irv – Jus hangin' out an' givin' ma brain a rest.

Roy – Yu been usin' yore brain a lot dese days?

Irv – Yep! Ah always do! ah tink 'bout stuff an' tink 'bout stuff an' tink 'bout stuff!

Roy – Wa stuff?

Irv – Oh! Will da sun come up? How long do nights last? Will de dress wif pink polkadots be wa ma girl-fren will wear next?

Roy – Ah dint kno' yu had a girl-fren. Wa's her name an wer's she frum?

Irv – Her name is *Dorothy* an' she's frum da *Wizard o' Oz!*

Roy – Ah asked yu a serious question an ah need a serious answer.

Irv – OK! Her name's *Rosemary* an' she's frum *Hoboken, New York.*

Roy – Wer's *Hoboken?*

    Irv – *Hoboken's* a suburb o' *New York City* in *Hudson County, New Jersey.* It has a population o' 59,000 an wa da birthplace o' *Frank Sinatra.*

Roy – Dat wa way more dan ah needed to kno'.

    Irv – Ah shud hab adjusted ma answer to da strenth o' yore brain.

Roy – Oh yeah? Yu ain' so smart either.

    Irv – Smarter'n yu!

Roy – Yeah? Wa's de square root o' 4.

    Irv – Ma smartness doesn' include *mathematics.*

Roy – Wat do it include?

    Irv – It include *baseball.*

Roy – OK! How many strikes til yore out?

    Irv – As many as yu can get away wif.

Roy – Yu any good at *fooo-a-ball?*

    Irv – Ah graduated at da top o' ma class in *fooo-a-ball.*

Roy – Wa hoppens wen yore tackled?

    Irv - Yu an' an yore opponent fall down wif arms an' legs in a tangled mess.

Roy – OK! Ah give up. Yu're smart in *fooo-a-ball* an' *base-a-ball*, but yu *cain't* play *chess*.

    Irv – Wyancha try me out?

Roy – OK! Here's a *chessboard* wif all da checkers. Wa de firs thing yu do?

    Irv – Dump it on de grass!

Roy – Maybe wen yore puttin' it away, but not if yore startin' a game.

    Irv - OK! So ah doan kno' how to play *chess*. Ah might say, *needer do yu!*

Roy – Ah confess. Yore right. Ah kno' nothin' o' chess. Ah wa jus' tryin' to trip yu up.

    Irv – Now dat yu've tripped yur-self up, wa ambush o' yu-self yu goin' to take next?

Roy – Less go eat somewer'. How 'bout *Hamburgeeny's Spaggeteeny* fo' hamburger and spaghetti?

Irv – Sounds horrible. Wa do dey hab fo' desert?

Roy – *Rumple de Dumple Icey-Cream* wif *Apple-De-Dapple Orangatange Pie.*

Irv – Das sumtin ah neva thoat o'.

Roy – Das wy eberybody goes to *Hamburgeeny's Spaggeteeny's.*

Irv – Jus' stick wif me. Ah'll take yu to de bes' eatin' places lak *Albergetti's Ding-Dong Betti's,* or *Carol Eats Dog, While in a Fog.*

Roy – Ah can' wait. Wen can we go'?

Irv – When de sun doan shine in de middle o' October.

Roy – Ah'll be ready.

Swordfish 14

Irv – Ah just got back frum *Idaho, Nebraska.*

Roy – Der ain' no *Idaho, Nebraska.* Thos'r two different *U. S. States.*

Irv – Well, Xcuse me! Dey ar' not! *Idaho's* da town an' *Nebraska's* da *State!*

Roy – Look on de map. It'll tell yu.

Irv – Here's de map. Ahm-a-lookin' it up! OK! Yore right!

Roy – Whoo's da dumb one now?

Irv – OK! So, ah'm de dumb one.

Roy – Ah tole yu, yu were de dumb one.

Irv – Between yu an' me, ah remember ah won de *Who's de Dumbest Contest.*

Roy - How well ah remember. Ah wa so delighted yu won.

Irv – How ja lak to hab a *Who's Smartest* Contest?

Roy – Ah hab no worries. Ah kno' who's smartest.

  Irv – Ah'm gonna ask de questions. Wa's de tallest buildin' in de worl'?

Roy – Da *Empire State Building* at 1,454-feet includin' antennas.

  Irv – Nope! *Burj Khalifa* at 2,717 feet. See? Ah'm smarter.

Roy – Wher' ju get dat info'?

  Irv – Offa de *Internet*.

Roy – Heck! Ah coulda done dat.

  Irv – But yu dint, an' ah won de *Contest*.

Roy – If yu tink yu did, das, good enuff, but not really.

  Irv – Who is de tallest *swordfish* in existence?

Roy – Doan yu mean de longest *swordfish* in existence?

  Irv – Yeah! Ah gess so, if yu hab to be so *pickity-unish*.

Roy – OK! So de *Internet* says most *sharkfish* is

longer dan a school bus, de longest being 40-feet.

Irv - No it aint! It's 62-feet long.

Roy - De 40-foot shark is a *Baskin' Shark*. Ah talkin' *Whale Shark*. Yu mixin' up da importance o' *Fish-Measurin'*.

Irv - Yu mean there's a *Whale Shark* an' a *Baskin Shark?*

Roy - Das how smart ah am.

Irv - Well, well! *Honky-Donk! Bless ma soul. Wish'd ah wer' a Donkey-Dole.*

Roy - Yu doan hab to make no joke out o' yore bein' dumb.

Irv - Cry! Ah wa-ned to be smart, an' ah'm jus not.

Roy - Yu're alive, tho. Das got to be *worth* sumptin.

Irv - Wud ah rather be here an' dumb or not be here an' not *smart or dum'?*

Roy - If yu were not here yu wudn't be *smart or dumb*.

Irv – Das wa ah said. Yu'd be non-existent, or in somebudies imagination. Or lak a move in a chess game wif no one to make it.

Roy – Now yu got it! Wa yu said wa really smart, though provoked by bein' dum'.

Irv – How 'bout ah singin' *"Goodbye ma Konie Island Baby?"*

Roy – How's it go?

Irv – *"Farewell, ma own tru luv. Ahma-gonn-ta sale away an' leeve yoooo. Neber to see yu any - - -"*

Roy – Was dat got to do wif anyting?

Irv – It wud add sum life to de *party*.

Roy – Der ain' no *party*.

Irv – Der is if we had some boooz!

Roy – OK! hab it yer own way! How de rest o' de song go?

Irv – Ah dunno'!

Monkey See, Monkey Do 15

Roy – As always ah'm gonna' open de discussion as ah sometimes do by askin' yu a quest-shun.

Irv – Go ahead. Ah kno' *eber-ting*.

Roy – Wa's da mos' impotant wish in yore whole life?

Irv – Is dat philosophic, psychologic or catch-me-in-a-joke?

Roy – Das ma problem. Yore's is to answer de quest-shun.

Irv – Gobblin' down a big piece o' *Blueberry Pie!*

Roy – Das all yu can tink o'?

Irv – Wa did yu Xpect? *Eberlastin Life? Married to a Movie Star? Winnin' de Horse Race at de Kentucky Derby.*

Roy – Cummin frum yu ah gess ah'm not surprised.

Irv – Wa wa de mos' impotant ting yu wish in yore life?

Roy – Winnin' de *Nobel Prize* fo' *English Literature*.

Irv – Yu ain' written no *prize-winnen* novels.

Roy – Ah would if ah tried.

Irv – Wy done yu try?

Roy – Ah'm scared.

Irv – Yu sposed to be de smart one an' yu doan eben *try* to fulfill yore *Dharma*.

Roy – Wa *Dharma?*

Irv – Yu sposed to be de smart one, an' yu doan kno' wa *Dharma* is?

Roy – *Monkey see, Monkey do!*

Irv – Yu not as smart as a *Monkey*.

Roy – Ah is too?

Irv – Is dis conversa-shun not 'bout *Monkeys Seein' & Doin'?*

Roy – Jus followin' yore lead.

Irv – How smart does a *Monkey* hab to be fo' president o' de *Unidy States?*

Roy – We already hab one runnin' rite now.

Irv – Ah kno' woo it is.

Roy – Ah kno' woo it is, too. Doan mention de name, cause we doan wan' to spred no rumors.

Irv – Ah won', 'cause ahm too polite.

Roy – Wa else is cookin'?

Irv – A half-o'-leg-o'-lamb.

Roy – Yu doan kno' how to roast lamb.

Irv – No! Ah wa jus' lyin' to be funny.

Roy – Das not funny. Try tellin' me anoder joke.

Irv – OK! Ah got plenty o' those. Wa did de snake say to de possum?

Roy – How do ah kno'? It's yore joke. Wa did de snake say to de possum?

Irv – *"Bet yu cain't crawl tru a tiny hole."*

Roy – Den wa hoppen?

Irv – Den de possum crawled in de hole.

Roy – So, das de joke?

Irv – No! de snake crawled in after him an' ate em.

Roy – Das not funny.

Irv – Gess' yu're right. It'd be tragic if yu care 'bout de *possum*.

Roy – If yu care 'bout de snake it might be *funny-er*.

Irv – Wa if yu doan care 'bout *smaller species*.

Roy – Den yu hab to stay out o' it, an' consider it jus' wa hoppens in our *Uni-berse* an' yu're stuck wif it.

Irv – Ah hate dat!

Girl-fren's 16

Roy – Yu neva talk 'bout yore *girl-fren*.

Irv – Ah tries to keep her private.

Roy – Wy fo' yu keep her private?

Irv – Cause she sometimes acks lak a *stick-in-de-dirt*.

Roy – Wy fo' yu say dat?

Irv – Cause ah'm embarrass'd.

Roy – Wa did she do now?

Irv – She run off de cliff wif ma moto-cycle an' wrecked de front end.

Roy – Is dat so bad?

Irv – Ah need to get a new motor-cycle.

Roy – Is dat de loaner yu been drivin' lately?

Irv - Das almos' de one.

Roy – Wa will it cos' yu?

Irv – A pig in a poke's ear.

Roy – How much is dat?

Irv – More dan ah make in a lifetime.

Roy – How much is dat'?

Irv - $2,463.00

Roy – Das not too bad.

Irv – Could yu len' me da money?

Roy – Yu already owe me a hun-derd bucks.

Irv – De loan would only be til *Saturday*. Den ah pay yu back wif interest.

Roy – How much wud be de interest?

Irv – Less dan ah'd make in a lifetime.

Roy – Ah doan make no interest in a lifetime.

Irv – Ah'll double dat'.

Roy – *Double O* is still *Double O*.

Irv – Das no concern o' mine.

Roy – No, Irv, ah'm not goin' to len yu one cent.

Irv – Den ah go wif-out a car.

Roy – An' *wif-out* a *Girl-fren*.

Irv – Ah needs ma *Girl-fren*.

Roy – Wa fo'?

Irv – To feel normal. lak a big *Dick*. de one woo people say, *"Looka dat! Irvin's actually got a Girl-fren."*

Roy – Kinda lak dey say 'bout me?

Irv – Yu ain' got no *Girl-fren*.

Roy – Yes ah do.

Irv – Wa her name?

Roy – *Claire Booth Luce*.

Irv – Das a writer's name.

Roy – OK! It's really *Patsy-Ann-Propeler*.

Irv – Lak de airplane?

Roy – Spelled wif one L.

Irv - Yu eva go flyin' wif her?

Roy - Ah went once, but not again.

Irv - Wy?

Roy - She fly so close to da hunderd story buildings, ah blew kisses at de *secretaries*.

Irv - Wat else she do?

Roy - She flew unner a low bridge an' her wheels touched water.

Irv - Wa else she do?

Roy - She did loop-de-loops in de air an' skidded sideways on de wings, dove at suicide speed to de top o' de ocean an' pulled up jus' befo smashin' into a tangled mess in de water an' sank.

Irv - Das enouff!

Irv – Ah jus got back fum bein' de *rain*.

Roy – Nobody does dat!

Irv – Ah done it!

Roy – How dya turn yursef into *rain?*

Irv – Magik words. *Hokey-Pokey Dominoke, Rain, Rain, Doan give me a Pain, Rata-tat-tat, Gimmee Yore Hat, ah tink ah Gotta Flat.*

Roy – Yu win de *Stupid Prize.* Wad-ja do while yu were *rain?*

Irv – Ah fell in gentle droplets on ma *girl-fren's* flowers, den as a torrent raced down de street lak a ribber.

Roy – Udder dan spellin' ribber wrong, das pretty cool. Is dat all yu did?

Irv – No! Later ah became an out-o'-cuntrol storm an' flooded a lake, dat broke a dam an' took out 14 homes.

Roy – Dint yu feel bad 'bout dat?

Irv - Wooo gonna blame de *rain?*

Roy – OK! Rain, Rain, Gimmee a Pain. *Hoke-Poke-Dominoke - Shazame!*

Irv – Yu ain' sposed to add *Shazame* after *Dominoke.*

Roy – No?

Irv – Yu should copy me Xactly! *Hokey-Pokey, Dominoke, Rain, Rain, Gimmee a Pain.* Den doan add no *Shazame* afterward.

Roy – Wa? How cum yu din turn into no *rain* when yu jus' said de *Magik Words?*

Irv - Perhaps, ah was'n tellin' de truth da firs' time.

Roy – Ah can bet ma bottom dollar yu woant tellin' de truth!

Irv – OK! Now ah'm goin' to turn ma-sef into *fog.* *Hankey - Pankey Ding - Dong - Crankey, Suddenly an' Quickly ah become a Hankey.*

Roy – Yu dint turn yurself into no *fog.*

Irv – So, ah'm not no *Magikian,* but if ah could turn ma-sef into a *Magikian* ah'd make ma-sef *fog*

an' float down de ribber an' hide fum de
birds.

Roy - Wy fo' yu'd hide fum de birds?

Irv - Cause das wa *fogs* do, not wa people do.

Roy - Yu got any more ignorant wishes?

Irv - Yeah! Ah'd lak to turn maself into de ocean.

Roy - How'd yu do dat?

Irv - *Sahmy-Dahmy, Dingleberry Namni, Hoochi-
Coochi Yu're a Moochy.*

Roy - No ah'm not!

Irv - Ah kno' yu're not. It's jus' *Magik* words.

Roy - Wa dat, de *Magik* formula fo' birds?

Irv - Cum to me little *Birdy-Poo. Inkley-Pinkley
Ombligoo, Folder Dobble Bottle-Poo-Screw
Yu.*

Roy - Boy! Yu sure nailed down dose *Magik* words.

Irv - It's part o' ma special genius.

Roy - OK! Wa if ah wanted to go fishin'?

Irv – *Sahmy-Dahmy's Goin' Fishin', Lion huntin', or Bird Watchin', or Bitten by-a buncha Mos-quit-tos.*

Roy – OK! Wa if ah wanted to go *Frog* Watchin'?

Irv – *To de Frog, say Tinky-Dinky, Mom's a Pinkey, Doan tel' Dad, Cause he's a Stinkey.*

Roy – Ders no *Frog.* Das no *Magik* words.

Irv – Lie enough an' yu soon believe yore lies.

Roy – Ah can see wer dat roole come frum.

Irv – Ah hate to take all da credit!

Burj Khalifa 18

Roy – Ringa-a-ting-a-ting.

Irv - Wa dat mean?

Roy – Das de sign o' a thoat bein' drummed up in de middle o' ma haid.

Irv - Wa de thoat?

Roy – Dat wat-ebers-up is not goin' down an' gonna be eva-lastinly OK.

Irv - Yu mean ahma gonna get ober ma drippy nose?

Roy – No! It ain' 'bout yu. If it wa ma drippy nose, ah might get ova it. If not ma nose, it's 'bout sumtin else.

Irv - Wa yu talkin' 'bout?

Roy – De *Ringa-ting-ting* thoat wer ahma goin' ta jump off o' da highest buildin' in da worl'.

Irv - Dat would be de *Burj Khalifa*, in Dubai, in de' country o' de *United World Emirates* das ova 2,700-feet tall.

Roy – Wer's da *United World Emirates?*

Irv – At de entrance to de *Persian Gulf.*

Roy – Wer's de *Persian Gulf?*

Irv – Near de *Red Sea.*

Roy – Wer's de *Red Sea?*

Irv – Heck! Ah doan kno'. It ain' 'round here.

Roy – Heck! Ah kno' it ain' 'round here. If it wa 2,700 feet tall, ah could see it frum here.

Irv – Speakin' about wa yu doan kno', hab yu seen any *squirrels* lately?

Roy – Ah had a nephew woo wa a little *squirrely.*

Irv – Ah'm not talkin' 'bout nutty nephews, ah'm talkin' 'bout real *squirrels.*

Roy – Wy fo' yu talkin' 'bout real *squirrels?* Yu soun' a little *squirrely* yur-suf.

Irv – Ah do lak peanuts, but dat isn' de reason.

Roy – Wats de reason yure tinkin bout *squirrels?*

Irv – Cause ma *girl-fren* got 2 pet *squirrels* an

she doan kno' wa to feed em.

Roy – Wy doan she get a book on dem?

Irv – An become sma't, lak me?

Roy – Yeah! Or me.

Irv – Yu ain' sma't.

Roy – Yeah! Ah am! Go ahead. As' me sumtin lak sma't.

Irv – Wa de capital o' *Canada?*

Roy – Ah doan kno'.

Irv – See? Ah tole yu yu wer not sma't.

Roy – Wa *IS* de capital o' *Canada?*

Irv – Ah doan kno', either. Das wy ah assed yu.

Roy – We gettin' nower fast.

Irv – Ah'l look it up on de *Internet.*

Roy – Yusin de *Internet* fo' brains, ah see?

Irv – De *Internet* says de capital o' *Canada* is *Ottawa* in de *South-east* portion o' de cuntry off de *Ottawa Ribber*.

Roy – Ah can see yu doan kno' how to spell ribber, either.

Irv – No! It's because yu doan kno' nuttin!

Roy – Ah got to get goin'. Ah got to jump off de *Burj Khalifa* tower at 2,700 feet high.

Irv – We all kno' yu ain' gonna do dat.

Roy – Yure right. De city council probably wouldn' wan' to clean up de sidewalk mess.

Irv – Wat yu be tinkin 'bout wile yu fallen 2,700 feet tru de air onto pavemen'?

Roy – How eberythin' gonna be OK!

De Water 19

Roy – Got anyting new to talk 'bout?

Irv – Ah jus' been de water.

Roy – Yu is a people. People doan get to *all-o'-a-sudden* be water.

Irv – Yu kno' dat fo' sure?

Roy – Eva budies kno's dat. Ah kno' it. Wat does dat tell yu?

Irv – Dat yu are a dumb-shit. Yu doan kno' eber-ting!

Roy – OK! Wa did yu do wile yu thoat yu wa water?

Irv – Not jus' give eber-budy a drink. No! Sumtin' much mo impotant dan dat. Sumtin' to make a possum yell *NO* while bein' trown off a airplane at 6,000-feet.

Roy – Wa dat?

Irv – Ah wa gonna be de whole ocean an' travel de worl'.

Roy – Isn' dat a bit *grandiose?*

   Irv – Ah suppose it is, considerin' ma self as bein' so little as compared to de 'hole *Uni-berse.*

Roy – Ah ain' comparin' yu.

   Irv – Ah din say yu wa. Wa am ah, a liar?

Roy – No! But yu gotta kno' yu sump-times stretch de troooth!

   Irv – While ah wa de ocean, ah swept 'round de end o' de continents goin' fast, lak rapids, 'cause ah'm higher on de *Pacific* side o' de continent dan on de *Atlantic* side due to de rotation o' de planet.

Roy – Wa?

   Irv – Yu din kno' de oceans on ea side o' de planet wer' at differnt levels?

Roy – Das not common kno'ledge.

   Irv - Well, das how it be. De *Lowd* say, yu mus' *re-ccept* de *inevitable.*

Roy – Wa else is *inevitable?*

   Irv – De sun cumin up. De win' blowin' hard. De hebby rains scourin de ocean, de tsunamis layin' waste to de land, de heat o' de desert, de volcanoes, de cole o' de artic. Ah thoat yu wa de smat one an' now ah see, instead, it's *ME*.

Roy – Heck! Ah thoat ah knew dat.

Irv – Den wy dju' ask?

Roy – *Eber-one's* not perfect.

Irv – Specially yu!

Roy – Ah'm perfeck in 'nother way.

Irv - Wa way is dat?

Roy – 'Long time ago, ma ancestors belonged to a cult named *Oooga Booo-Booo Saanda Dooo-Dooo, Dingy-Dongy, Scubby Looo-Looo.*

Irv – Das a dum' title.

Roy – Dey believed *Nuf-fin'* dat *Neber Wa*, wa *Sum-tin'* dat *Always Wa.*

Irv – *Nuf-fin'* dats *Sump-tin'?*

Roy – Dey believed if yu hab *Nuf-fin,'* dat *Nuf-fin'* is *Sump-tin'.*

Irv – No, it's not.

Roy – If yu *DOAN* hab a penny, den de penny yu doan hab *is SUMP-TIN'* yu doan hab.

Irv – Yu mean *MONEY* ah don' hab is de *SUMP-TIN'* ah hab?

Roy – Yu hab de basis o' de belief, dat *NUF-FIN'* is *SUMP-TIN'*.

Irv – Ah could belong to dat cult. Ah ain' got *Nuf-fin'*, but it sure feels good to hab *Sump-tin'*, eben if it cain't pay no debts.

Roy – Yu can see monetarileee, it's a useless rule, but not bein' too critical, ah can see dat in some unkno'n fassion, ah feel better.

Irv – Yu tink yure gonna take up dat cults philosophy?

Roy – Yes! Wa eva ma ansestors tink is right fo' me to tink.

Irv – Ah kin see if yu believe *Nuf-fin'* *is Sump-tin'* yure cut frum de mold.

Roy – Das de nicest ting yu eva sed to me.

Irv – Ah'm a convicted liar.

Roy – Yu tink yure a *magician.*

    Irv – Ah kno' ah'm a *magician.*

Roy – Prove it to me! *Walk tru dat Wall.*

    Irv – Heck! Give me sump-tin' hard to do. Dat too easy.

Roy – Jus' *Walk tru dat Wall.*

    Irv – *Walk. Walk. Boomp! Boomp! (Fall down.)*

Roy – See? Yu cudn't do it. Yu jus' fell down an' *booomped* yore haid.

    Irv – Let me try it, again. Ah wa jus' out o' practice. *Walk. Walk. Boomp! Boomp! (Fall down.)*

Roy – See? Dat oughta' prove it to ya. Yooo ain' no magician.

    Irv – Ah could turn a *Bollen Ball* into a *Tomato.*

Roy – De heck yu cud.

    Irv – Give me a *Bollen Ball.*

Roy – Ah doan hab no *Bollen Ball*.

  Irv – OK! Den, *Tennis Ball*!

Roy – Ah doan hab no *Tennis Ball*.

  Irv – How 'bout an *Apple*.

Roy – Yu goan turn an *Apple* into a *Bollen Ball?*

  Irv – No! Ah goan turn it into a *Tomato.*

Roy – Here's de *Apple*.

  Irv – Irv trow's de *Apple* in de air an' it falls to de' floor an' rolls under a chair.

Roy – Ah got more importan' tings to do. Ah'm wastin' ma time.

  Irv – OK! Ahm takin' lessons to be a magician. Today de lesson is, ah gonna *Jump off a Bridge*.

Roy – How high de *Bridge?*

  Irv – 95 feet.

Roy – Yu'll kill yoreself!

  Irv – No! Dey's a trick ah'm spposed to learn.

Roy – Wa dat?

Irv - Ah speeks some crazy words lak *La La Paloooza, dis is a Dooza, Boggle de Mind an' Tickle ma Dooza.* Or sumtin lak dat an' de custimoor doan see wat really happens.

Roy – Better make sure de words doan boggle yore own mind. Yu might magician yur-self off de bridge an' fall to *ignominies* death wif no one to save yore scrawny hide.

Irv – Yu tink ma instructor is dat dumb – or *ignominies,* wa-eber dat means. Wa should ah do?

Roy – *Fire de Re-instructor.*

***Instructor* Irv** – Wa! *Fire ME?* Ah'll hab yu kno' ah'm de mos' famos' *Instructor* dis side o' de *Mississippi Ribber.*

Roy – Yu spelled *ribber* wrong. Wy 'nt yu show me a magical trick, lak *Walkin' on de Ceiling.*

***Instructor* Irv** – Ah would, cept ah doan hab no *Magic Shoes.*

Roy – Wa if yu had yore *Magic Shoes?*

***Instructor* Irv** - Den ah'd walk all ober de ceiling

an' walls an' trees an' clouds an' mountains an'
de railroad tracks an' eber-wer.

Roy - How about alongside ma car on de way to yore
home?

Irv - How dare yu in-sult ma *special magician -
ship?*

Roy - He needs insultin'! His ego's so big, it's affectin'
his mind.

Irv - Ah tink Roy's right. Ah've not learned a ting
fo' all yu've told me. Ah cain't eben walk tru
a door wif-out booompin' ma haid.

Instructor **Irv** - Yu were a pretty no-good
student frum wer ah stood.

Roy - It's time fo' yu to leave.

Instructor **Irv** - Cain't wait to go.

Roy - Doan take no *wooden nickels.*

Irv – Now ah'm a *Mountain*.

Roy – Yu tink yure eber-ting.

Irv – No! Dis time, ah'm really a *Mountain*.

Roy – Wy do yu tink yu're a *Mountain*.

Irv –Cause ah'm big an' fat on de bottom an' come to a point at de top.

Roy – So do de *Mountains*, but *Mountains* doan breath, or do push-ups, or hab bad breath, or *Fart*.

Irv – So? Ah may hab an *imperfectshun* or two.

Roy – Yu got arms an' legs an' eat food. Yu lak *Blueberry Pie*. As far as *Mountains* is concerned yu has many im-per-fect-shuns.

Irv - *Blueberry Pie* is one ting ah do lak.

Roy – Wan' some now?

Irv – Ah believe ah do.

Roy – *Mountains* doan lak *Pie.*

   Irv – How yu kno'? Yu ain' been no *Mountain.*

Roy – Yu ain' neither! Maybe in yore mind yu once wa a *Mountain.*

   Irv – Wa rong wif ma mind?

Roy – Nuf-fin' - if yu got one.

   Irv – Yu're sayin' ah doan hab no mind?

Roy – No! Yu got one alright, it jus' ain' big ennuff.

   Irv – Oh? Ah suppose yu got a big mind.

Roy – Big enough to kno' ah'm not a *Mountain.*

   Irv – Ah got a mind as big as a *Mountain.*

Roy – Maybe as big as yore *Stomach.*

   Irv – Big *Stomach's* are good fo' digestin' *Blueberry Pie.*

Roy – At least yu're' good fo' sump-tin' – if yu lak *Blueberry Pie.*

   Irv – Ah lak udder tings, too.

Roy – Wa?

    Irv – Smash'd potatoes, corn on de cob, cranberry sauce, ice cream, twinkly little do-do's sprinkled at random over a fluffy chocolate cake.

Roy – Eber-budy do! Dat proves yore *Human* an' not a *Mountain*.

    Irv – Ah doan need no *proof*.

Roy – Den wa yu got?

    Irv – Ah got *Faith!*

Roy – Yu got *Faith* yore a *Mountain?*

    Irv – Yeah!

Roy – Ah got *Faith* yu're not no *Mountain*.

    Irv – Mah *Faith* is so strong, ah doan tink yu hab *Faith*. Ah tink ah'm an *Angel*.

Roy – An *Angel* frum *God?*

    Irv – Yep! Ah wa sent here to save de worl'.

Roy – Yu tink de worl' need savin'?

Irv – Looka all de *Candy* in de *Candy* stores.

Roy – Yu gonna get rid o' *Candy?*

Irv – No! *Blueberry Pie* is kinda lak *Candy*.

Roy – But it's not 'Xactly lak *Candy?*

Irv - No! Das wy ah eat it.

Roy – Is eatin *Candy* de only way yu gonna save de worl'?

Irv – No! Ah'm gonna stop *skateboardin'*, too.

Roy – Yu tink dats bad fo' de worl'?

Irv – Yu could break an ankle. Ah'm 'gainst playin' *Marbles*, too!

Roy – Wy yu 'gainst dat?

Irv – Yu cuud dislocate yore thumb or get yore knees scratched if yore kneelin' down an' wen pants wore out, or lose all yore *Marbles* an' go home cryin'.

Roy – Ah can see yore point.

Round de Worl' 22

Irv – Here's de top o' ma list.

Roy – Wa dat?

Irv – Ah goin' *sail* 'roun de worl'.

Roy - How yu gonna' go, take a plane, take a boat, take a train, or go hitch-hiken?

Irv – Ahma gonna' take de car.

Roy – Yu said yu gonna *SAIL* 'roun de worl'?

Irv – Yu rite! Ah ain' gonna *SAIL* aroun' de worl', ah gonna *DRIVE* 'roun de worl'.

Roy – Make up yu're mind. Ar' yu gonna *SAIL* or *DRIVE* roun de worl'?

Irv – Ah'm a free person. Ah'm gonna *WALK* roun de worl'.

Roy – How yu gonna *WALK* on water. Yu gonna' *sink-lak-a stone*. De fish'll eat yu up.

Irv – Der may be a few kinks in ma plan.

Roy – Eaten by fish shu'd not be one o' em.

  Irv – How 'bout ah go by *Balloon?*

Roy – Dey's no way to steer a *Balloon*. Yu'd be blown all de way to *Australia*, den de Souf pole an' trampled to death by penguins.

  Irv – Yu're so negative. How 'bout ah *Rollerskate?*

Roy – Yore scates'll wear out.

  Irv – How 'bout ah *Springboard Dive?* Ah'm good at dat.

Roy – Der ain' no swimmin' pools wif divin' boards all roun' de worl'.

  Irv – Gess yu're rite.

Roy - Yu a crazy mixed up kid who doan kno' der *Toozy* frum der *Doozy*.

  Irv – Ah do too.

Roy – Wa's a *Toozy* an' a *Doozy?*

  Irv – Ah doan kno'.

Roy – Ah jus' made dis up. A *Toozy* is yore *Haid* an' a *Doozy* is yore *Butt.*

Irv – In other words, ah doan kno' ma *Haid* frum ma *Butt?*

Roy – Now yu're cookin' wif *kerosene.*

Irv – Das not fair.

Roy – Den give up dis crazy idea 'bout sailin' or walkin' 'roun de worl'.

Irv – Yeah! Ah doan hab no money, anyway.

Roy – Go to de picture show wif me. Ah'll pay.

Irv – Yu got de money?

Roy – Ah jus' got paid frum workin' at de liquor store sellin' alcohol-candy to minors.

Irv – How much dey pay yu?

Roy – $10.

Irv – Das pretty *Re-spensive.*

Roy – Better dan a poke in de eye wif a sharp violin.

Irv – Wa we gonna see?

Roy – *Goin' Down de Hill doin' 90 Miles an Hour.*

Irv – OOOeeee! Dat sounds exciting. Wa wer' dey
to meet at de bottom o' de hill?

Roy – Ah doan kno'. Leopard sharks in a pool swirln'
fo' food, a herd o' elephants tramplin' down
a forest, a bunch o' sharks tarin' up a criminal
dats escapen in de water? Ah doan kno'.

Irv – Ah cain't wait. Ah jus' luv's movies!

Roy - *Sally* an' *Margie* are goin' wif us.

Irv – We goin' wif dates?

Roy – It's all set up.

Irv – Ah jus' loves *Margie*.

Roy – She lak's yu, toooo. But she's leavin' fo' Idaho.

Blueberry Pie 23

Irv – Ah jus' loves *Jarma*.

Roy – Is-zat yore new girl-fren?

Irv – No! Dat's a new way o' *philo-so-fizin'*.

Roy – Yu mean *Djarma* - De eternal truth. De right way o' libin.

Irv – Das it!

Roy – Wa do yu kno' 'bout *Djarma?*

Irv – Nuf-fin'

Roy – Ah figured dat.

Irv – Ah jus' loves *Djarma* cause its de right way o' libin.

Roy – Long de way, *Djarma* has ben given good points.

Irv – Ah gonna unner-stan' dose. How do ah get *Djarma?*

Roy – Yu gotta' go deeper dan desire.

Irv – Wa?

Roy – Yu cain't just desire stuff, yu gotta hab *aspiration.*

Irv – Wa? Yu gotta breath fast, or sump-tin'?

Roy – No, fast-breathin' is 'nother type o' *Djarma.* Yu hab to develop *aspira-shun,* wich is de hope or *ambi-shun* o' achievin' some important life work, or sump-tin'.

Irv – Das it?

Roy – *Aspira-shun* means wa do yu wanna *aspire* to?

Irv – Ah wanna *aspire* to eatin' *Blueberry Pie.*

Roy – Yu should be der now. Dat wud be buyin' a *Blueberry Pie* den eatin' it, not *aspirin'* to become a *Blueberry Pie.*

Irv – Cud yu len me da money to buy ma *aspira-shuns?*

Roy – Lendin' yu money ain' *Djarma.*

Irv – Howma gonna get de *Blueberry Pie?*

Roy – Borrow de money frum de bank.

Irv – Dey put me ona *wanted* list.

Roy – Since yore on a *wanted* list, ah gess yu ought to hold off on borrowin' frum de bank.

Irv – Ah better ask *Aunt Polly* fo' de money.

Roy – She ain' gonna give it to yu since yu crashed her car.

Irv – Oh yeah! Ah forgot 'bout ah crashed her car.

Roy – Forget 'bout de *Blueberry Pie*. In yore mind, hole de *aspira-shuns* fo' de future munchin' down an' swallowin' o' de *Blueberry Pie*.

Irv – Ah kno' wa ah'll do.

Roy – Wa?

Irv – Ah'l bake ma own.

Roy – Yu kno' how to bake a *Pie?*

Irv – No! But ah cud' learn.

Roy – Wa yu hab to do firs'?

Irv – Get de *materials*.

Roy – Wher yu gonna get de *materials*.

Irv – Buy em. Oh, wait! Ah doan hab no money.

Roy – Das cause yu're a dumb-ass.

   Irv – Ah mite be dumb, but it's not only ma ass das dumb.

Roy – It's yore haid, too.

   Irv – Wa should ah be wantin'?

Roy – De true meaning o' *Djarma*.

   Irv – Wa dat?

Roy – Ah tole yu. De eternal truth. de rite way o' libin.

   Irv – How ah get dat?

Roy – By goin' deeper an' deeper an' thru intense *aspira-shun*.

   Irv – Yu mean ah got to do more *fast-breathin'*?

Roy – No! Yu hab to fine yore *aspira-shun*, if yu got any, wich ah suspect yu ar' as far away frum dat as de *Souf Pole*.

Ah Wanna Play Music 24

Irv – Ah wanna play music!

Roy – Well, go ahead an' play it!

Irv – Ah doan kno' how.

Roy – Looks lak yu gotta take sum lessons. Wa instrument yu gonna play?

Irv – Ah doan kno'. Sump-tin' musical dat'll play tings lak *Wait Til de Sun Shiins Snellly*.

Roy – Das an ole tune. Doan yu wanna play sump-tin classical lak *Beethoven's Symphony in D-flat Minor or F-sharp Major or L-Indistinguishable Dull* or sump-tin' lak dat?

Irv – Naw!

Roy – Ah can see yu doan hab no musical education.

Irv – Ah'm not impressed wif yore's, either.

Roy – Ah neber said ah wa much o' a *musician*.

Irv – Ah neber heard o' *L-Indistinguishable Dull* befor'.

Roy – It's possible der insn' any.

Irv – Believe me, der isn' any.

Roy – Now yu're de expert.

Irv – It sure ain' yu!

Roy – Ah neber said ah wa. Ah repeat, wa instrumen' yu gonna' play?

Irv – Ah lak *Crackerjack*.

Roy – Der ain' no instrumen' called *Crackerjack*.

Irv – Ah thought der wa.

Roy – Yu tinkin o' *Popcorn*. Dey make *Crackerjack* out o' *Popcorn*.

Irv – Yu're right. Ah mustav ben rememberin' music fo' sumtin ah ate. OK! Forget *Cracker-jack*.

Roy – Desert an' *Dirt* an' music ar' easy to mistake.

Irv – Tank yu fo' yu kindness. OK! Den ah lak an *Instrument* called *Peaner Butter an' Jelly*.

Roy – Das food, again. *Peaner Butter an' Jelly* ain' no musical instrument, an' befor yu bring it up, needer is *Blueberry Pie*.

Irv – Sorry! Wa instrument shud ah play?

Roy – Yu're de one woose all hot an' ding-donged 'bout tanglin' yoresef up wif music. Das fo' yu to deside.

Irv – Ah pick sump-tin dat goes *Rata-Tat-Tat, Pinka-a-Doodle-Scat,* ah'm a *Little Cookie* dat goes *Pit-Pit-Pat.*

Roy – Der ain' no instrumen' dat does dat. Dat shows me yu cain't do *Doodley-Squat* to help yore sef do *Ding-Dong.*

Irv – Yu're right. OK! Ah pick de drums, an' ah gonna beat on de desk Wif a *Ding-Dong-Poo, Anna Doodle-de-Do, til de Cows go Moo!*

Roy – Das more lak it. Ah kin get behind somebody wooo has de spark o' lightinin' to knock me or any other leader in de haid an' out o' de *neighborhood.*

Irv – Ah doan tink ah got dat much.

Roy – Ah probably am overstatin' ma case, but yu're still a good fren.

Irv – Yu really mean dat Roy?

Roy – Ah wa neber more sincere, since ah lied 'bout brakin' ma mother's *irre-place-able* vase.

   Irv – Ah remember dat. Yu wa a little tinker. *(Tinker is Stinker)*

Roy – Ah remember yu in de ol' days. Yu throwed a baby alligator into de washing machine an' scared *Gramma* who turned wite an' trew up in de sink.

   Irv – An yu, Roy, throw'd a cat into a mouse cage dat only got pulled out jus' in time to save de mouses untimely deth.

Roy – Wy yu gonna save mice?

Dingleberry 25

Roy – Jus' got back fum mowin' de lawn an, boy, wa it a *Ding-Dong*.

Irv – Wa yu mean *Ding-Dong?*

Roy – Ah mean *Rump-de-Dump* or *Scally-Wag-Woo-Woo*, giv' it up fo' *Dump-Yur-Sauce Doo-Doo!*

Irv – Ah give up.

Roy – *Ding-Dong* or *Scally-Wag* is differnt names fo', *Tuff* or *Downrite Disturbin'*.

Irv – Wy din yu say mowin' de lawn wa *Tuff or Disturbin'* in de firs' place?

Roy – Jus' tryin' to match de level o' yore brain.

Irv – Ah'll hab yu kno' ah graduated wif de highest honors - mostly in *English*.

Roy – Wa dju get all *D's* in yore classes?

Irv – No! Ah got all *L's* an' *M's*.

Roy – Der ain' no *L & M* grades.

Irv – Der wa at ma *School.*

Roy – Wa *School* d-ju go to?

Irv – *Blueberry Pie High School.*

Roy – Ah always thought der wa a reason yu wer' a *Blueberry Nut.*

Irv – Yu wud be, too, if yu lak'd *Blueberry Pie* as much as ah do.

Roy – Wa 'bout *Dingle-Berry Pie?*

Irv – Wer do *Dingle-Berries* come fum?

Roy – Fum de *Dingle-Berry* tree, on de *East Coast o' America.*

Irv – Der ain' no *Dingle-Berry* Tree dat ah kno' o'.

Roy – Check de *Internet.* See? It has kind o' a *Cranberry Fruit* yu cud make into a pie, tho ah wou'nt want to mistake it fo' de odder meaning o' *Dingle-Berries.*

Irv – One, two - *Button ma Shooo.*

Roy – Wy yu say dat?

Irv - Tired o' dis subjeck.

Roy – Ma shoes is already buttoned. No! Dey doan hab no buttons, dey jus' hab laces. One, two, *Lace-Up-Ma Shooos*. Eben if it doan rhyme.

Irv – Doan yu tink de ocean is *polluted* enough?

Roy – It's *polluted* almost to de maximum.

Irv - Ah gonna *polute* it eben mo.

Roy – How yu gonna dat?

Irv – Tro ma *unner-wear* in da ocean.

Roy – It gonna be *dirdy unner-wear?*

Irv – Course it will. Ah gonna trow in las weeks *unner-wear.*

Roy – Wy-fo' yu gonna do dat?

Irv – Cause ah'm a stinky pig.

Roy – Ah gonna report yu to de fish in de water.

Irv – Fish doan hab no judges.

Roy – If dey cud talk dey could hab law schools.

Irv – No dey cudn't! Wer de school be?

Roy – Ova by de unner-watter cavern.

Irv – Yu mean near *Hawthorne Street?*

Roy – Yu kno' wer dat is?

Irv – Jus' 'cross frum de park.

Roy – Wa park?

Irv – *Pacific Ocean Park.*

Roy – Dey ain' no *Pacific Ocean Park.* Specially in de *Pacific Ocean.*

Irv – Well, it sure ain' goan be in de *Atlantic Ocean.*

Roy – Dis a nonsense discussion.

Irv – Yu rite, less quit.

New Religion 26

Irv – Yu got religion?

Roy – Ah got ma own kine o' religion.

Irv – Wa dat?

Roy – Be a happy-go-lucky guy dat doan get pissed off eber five minutes an' scream a buncha problems dat push people into fights. Wy? Wa religion yu got?

Irv – Mah new religion is *Blueberry Pie*.

Roy – Das a food!

Irv - It's still *Blueberry Pie!*

Roy – Ah neber knew any religion yu cud eat.

Irv – Maybe ah single-handedly invented de first religion in de hole worl' dat yu cud actually eat.

Roy – Dat's good, an' all, but people tink o' religions as a *personal philosophy*.

Irv – Cain't yu imagine goin' into a church, an'

after choir, de pastor bring out a slew o' half-sized *Blueberry Pies* fo' eber-one in de church to munch down?

Roy – Churches caint afford dat! Church's are to re-mine people o' a way o' life.

   Irv – Ah be better off if ah had bodily nourishment.

Roy – Churches ar' bigger dan food.

   Irv – Not fo' de homeless!

Roy – Yu sposed to hab *Pie* at home.

   Irv - Ah neber get any.

Roy – If yu had a *Moma*, yu'd get some.

   Irv – Moma doan gib me none.

Roy – Ask her, den.

   Irv – When ah ask, *"Ma, kin ah hab sum Blueberry Pie?"* She say, No! Get outa ma kitchen an' doan come back til yu're stavin to deth.

Roy – OK! Go ahaid wif yore *Blueberry Pie Religion*. It's probably as good as any.

Irv – Tanks, Roy, ah really appreciate yore *Xtreme generosity.*

Roy – Tanks Irv. Yore *English* is as bad as mine.

Irv – *"Copy Me, Copy Do."* Ah'ma gonna write yu up in ma records as de only approvin' member o' ma *Blueberry Pie Religion.*

Roy – Yu, doan hab ta do dat!

Irv – No! Ah want to. Wa better dan to hab a pal who lies 'bout yore *Religion.*

Roy – Dat's not all ah lie 'bout.

Irv - Wa else yu lie 'bout?

Roy – Ah lie 'bout yore jaunty style, yore ease wif people, yore generally bein' a good guy.

Irv – How 'bout ma intellect?

Roy – Yu ain' perfect! As ah've noticed, yu hab no brains,

Irv – Yu mean ah'm a dumb-ass?

Roy – Well, yu did cum up wif *Blueberry Pie Religion.* Das not 'Xactly brilliant.

Irv – Well, screw yu!

Roy – Screw yu, too!

Irv – After ah made yu an honorary, if only, member o' ma *Blueberry Pie Religion*, yu say, *"Screw yu?"*

Roy – As ah see it, ah speak de troooth.

Irv – Das de las' time ah gonna defulge ma long lost *Blueberry Pie Religion* to yu.

Roy – In de firs' place, ah dint ask yu to.

Irv – Ah'm neber, neber, neber gonna do it again.

Roy – Dat soun' lak a song, ma mudder toat to me

Inner Self 27

Roy – Well, wa yu gonna say now?

Irv – Ah'ma given in to ma *inner* self.

Roy – Ah'v herd 'bout de *inner* self. Yu got one?

Irv – Eber-budy got one.

Roy – Wer' is it?

Irv – It's *inside* da body.

Roy – Yu mean yore body holds somtin dats not yu?

Irv – Yore *inner self IS* yu.

Roy – Ah neva herd o' it?

Irv – Mos' people neva knew dey had an *inner self.*

Roy – Wa'd dey tink wa in der?

Irv – Not de *Lone Ranger*, or not *De Man Wif de Iron Potato*, or not *Snow Wite an' de Seben Giants*.

Roy – Eber-budy 'nows dey isn' dose people. Wa *IS* de *inner self?*

Irv – Yursef 'bout whom yu'll neber be aware.

Roy – Lak ah might say, *Howdee! Mr. Inner Person. Gladda meetcha.* Who de heck are yu?

Inner Self says – Ah'm de hidden person behind de person yu tink yu is. Gladda meetcha. *Howdee Doo-Doo. Polly-Crackers. Sorry fo' de Kraken Poo-Poo.*

Roy – Den ah might say. Ah doan kno' wooo de person is dat is yu - dat might be me.

Inner Self says – Ah is quite a mystry. Yu kin fine out 'bout me thru dreams.

Roy – Ah dreamed ah wa a bird flyin' ober *Africa* wen a thunderstorm burst on ma wings an' ah fell lak a stone into de ragin' waters o' a violent storm dat broke on once-calm waters, but now on jagged rocks.

Inner Self says – Das pretty poetic. It shows yu goin' 'long, mindin' yore own business, wen sump-tin yu din re-pect dropped on yu an' tru yu off, trippin' and fallen, on yo face.

Roy – Wa am ah spossed to do wif dat *scenario?*

Inner Self says – Yu sposed to fine out wat de ting wa' dat tru yu off balance an into a tizzy.

Roy – Ah kno's wa it is.

Irv – Wa is it?

Roy – *Ma divorce!*

Irv – Yu married?

Roy – Not any more. Tings wer' goin' to tangled snakes in a foot-casket an' we had to dump de marriage befo' it whacked us boff on de noggin' lak bein' dropped lak a six-pound bag o' oranges wen tryin' to 'scape bein' hit by a bus.

Irv – Dat soun' serious! Yu tink yu did de rite ting?

Roy – *Yowsa-Bowsa! Right-O-Bowsa.* Dat lowed me to meet *Georgia.*

Irv – Yu lak *Geogia?*

Roy – De cats howl in de night, an doan take *Ding-Dong* frum a *Wadayacallit.*

Irv – She soun' OK! See wat findin' yore *inner self* say fo' yu?

Roy – Is dat wa it does?

   Irv – Wanna do it again?

Roy – Dere's more?

   Irv - After havin' only one divorce, yu din tink yu were perfeck, did yu?

Roy – Ah thoat one marriage wa enough.

   Irv – People hab had many divorces many times. Dey've had a *Plethora* o' divorces.

Roy – Der's dat word ah doan kno' called *Plethora*. Wat do it mean?

   Irv – It means yu ar' a dumb-ass an' doan kno' de *English Language*.

Roy – Ah do too.

   Irv – Den wats *Plethora* mean?

Roy – Heck! Ah doan kno'.

Strung-Up 28

Roy – Halo! Halo! Halo!

Irv – Wa yu so happy 'bout?

Roy – Jus' got an inheritance frum an unkno'n relative frum a different country ah neva herd o' in mah life befo'.

Irv – Well! Das sump-tin'. Ah always wished sump-tin' lak dat wud' happen to me, but ah gess ma wishes ar' nuttin but *Meaningless Trow-Away Fancies o' a Mind Slowly Losin' a Plethora o' Faculties.*

Roy – Yu been losin' *Plethora* fo' years.

Irv – Jus' cause yore rich doan meen yu're smart. How much d-ju get?

Roy – Amma notta kno' til ma lawyer calls me up an' givs me de figures.

Irv – Ah hope it's enough to lend me a few bucks til Saturday.

Roy – Ah'm always lendin' yu money. Wen yu gonna quit askin' me?

Irv – Wen de snow falls deep in *West Africa* an' ma girl-fren whispers sweet no-buddy's into ma elbow insted o' a pillow.

Roy – Ah takes dat as neva, wich is wa ah suspected. Course if ah get a million bucks, yu can hab de 10 til *Saturday.*

Irv – Tanks a lot. Ah'll jus' *Wait fo' de Day.*

Roy - De money spossed to come *delibbered* by hoss-back.

Irv – Wy doan dey send it by mail?

Roy – Sump-tin' to do wif *Regulations.*

Irv – Tink Ah'll get into de mailin' business.

Roy – Dat goin' to be yore *Djarma?*

Irv - Yeah! Tink ah'll hab a new *Djarma* called *deliverin' mail.*

Roy - Gotta tink careful 'bout *Djarma.* Once yu get into it yu is tide-up lak a *ham-string-knot.*

Irv – Wa's *ham-string-knot?*

Roy – Strung-up lak yu wa a future ham fo' dinner an' now all ham-strung an' in de frigeratory danglin' on a cold hook.

Irv – Not strung-up lak a cow's-leg?

Roy – Ah'm no expert. Could be strung ova de shoulder lak a six-shooter *gun-in-a-holster*.

Irv – We doan wanna get violent, do we?

Roy – Ah not gettin' violent, jus' lookin' at de *rank possibilities*.

Irv – If yu use *gun-in-holster*, it soun' *rank* to me.

Roy – Ah take it back. How'd we get into a gun discussion?

Irv – We talkin' 'bout *Djarma*, an' all dat led to guns.

Roy – Ah remember. Yu might hab made de rong choice an' picked de rong *Djarma*.

Irv – Man picks de rong *Djarma* an' trows away his hole life!

Roy – Das stretchin' it. It jus' means be sure when it comes to pickin' a *Djarma*.

Irv - Ah'm as sure as ma Mom callen me to dinner.

Roy – Wa yu habin?

Irv – *Colly-Flower Soup* an' *Salt-Sprinkled Corn-Flops.*

Roy – Dat soun good. Kin ah cum?

Irv – Sure, if yu bring yore roller skates.

Roy – Wy ah hab to bring roller skates?

Irv – To roller-skate down de hill on our block.

Roy – Howja get dat?

Irv – Landslide!

Roy – Dat's too bad!

Irv – Buried ma bedroom, too.

Roy – Dat's terrible!

Irv – Mom says de *Colly-Flower Soup* an' *Sprinkled Corn-Flops* ar' still on!

Pop-Singer

Irv – Ah wanna be a *Pop-Singer*.

Roy – Das pretty hard iffen yu doan hab no re-sperience. Ah s'ppose yu doan wanna be a *Pop-Corn-Singer?*

Irv – No! Ah'm tinkin o' a more musical *Pop-Singer*, rather dan a *Pop-Corn-Singer* yu might eat at a pick-shure show.

Roy – Wa kind wud dat be?

Irv – How 'bout *Way Down 'Pon de Swannee Ribber*.

Roy – Besides spellin' *Ribber* 'rong, *Swannee Ribber's* been done! How 'bout *Pop-Goes-de-Weasel?*

Irv – Ah neva herd o' dat song.

Roy – Ah doan tink der is one.

Irv – Yu got any udder ideas?

Roy – *Pop Goes de Gun - When it Shoots Off,* dat is.

Irv – How yu gonna sing 'bout a *Gun Poppin'-Off?*

Roy – Pretty hard ah suspect.

Irv – Ah thoat 'bout a great big *Pop*, lak de explosion o' a buildin' blowin' up, but doan kno' how to make a song out o' it.

Roy – Yu cud make a song out o' *Poppin'* fo' a gift. Or *Poppin'* into another room, or *Poppin'* out-o-tha bathroom or *Poppin'* into or outa o' a marriage. *(Poppin', dat is, not Poopin')*

Irv – Der's a *Plethora* amount o' ways to use *Pop.*

Roy – Wat do *Plethora* mean?

Irv - Ah tole yu already. *Plethora* is not *Skinny Paluzza*, but *Lots-a-Paluzza!*

Roy – Oh yeah! Ah remember. Instead o' bein' a *Pop-Singer* wyn't ya be a *Pethora-Singer?*

Irv - Das crazy. *Plethora dis, Plethora dat, Won't yu be ma Plethora Girl-fren.* Cud ah make a song outa it?

Roy – At least it's differnt. Yu be de firs' person in de hole' worl' to sing a song 'bout his *Plethora* o' *Girl-fren's.*

Irv – Das a good idea. Ah lak de *Girl-fren Idea*, especially a *Plethora* o' em.

Roy – Yu cud start a *Plethora-Club* o' *Girl-fren's*. *Eben de Girls* might lak it.

Irv – Yu mean jus' forget de idea o' bein' a *Pop-Singer* an' be a *Plethora-Singer?*

Roy – *Girl-fren, Girl-fren, Won't yu be ma Plethora-Girl-fren.* Tink o' de tings dat rhyme wif *Plethora*.

Irv – Wa?

Roy – Sarah, Clara, tempora, Leonora, flora, Nora, Enora, Theodora, etc. Deys a *Dink-Pot* full o' rhymin' words.

Irv – Naw! Ah doan lak de idea!

Roy – Cause it's not yurs. Yu're jus' *jealous!*

Irv – Ah is not! Ah jus' want to be *creative*.

Roy – Ah thought yu wanted to be a *Pop-Singer*.

Irv – Oh yeah! Ah forgot.

Roy – Yu cudn't hab wat yu wanted very bad if yu already forgot.

Irv – Gess yu're right.

Roy – Wa yu really wanna be, now dat yu've thoat 'bout it?

Irv – Ah wanna *Roool de Worl'*.

Roy – Das too much trubel. Dat doan make no sense. Dat crazy!

Irv – Wa wud yu lak to be kno'in yu doan kno' how? lak bein' somebody, an' establishin' woo yu ar'?

Roy – Ah'd search fo' ma *Djarma*.

Irv – *Djarma, Djarma, Won't yu be ma Djarma Boy.*

Roy – *Djarma* means yore true callin' in life.

Irv – Wa dat?

Roy – Nobody kno's.

Let Me Call Yu Sweetheart 30

Roy – *L – L – Let me call yu Sweeetheaart, ah'm in Luv Wif Choooo.*

Irv – Yeah! Ah kno'. *L – L – Let me hear yu Wisss-perrr Dat Yu Luv Me Tchooooo!*

Roy – *Keeeep-a-Da Love-a-Lite Burnin' in Yore Heart so Truooo, Truooo Truooo. . .*

Irv – *Let-a-Me-Call yu a Sweet-a-Heart Ah – Ah – Ah'm in a-Luv Wif Tchoooo. . .*

Roy – Waja tink o' dat song, Irv?

Irv - Ah wa neber sure yu felt dat way 'bout me.

Roy – Snot 'bout yu. It's 'bout me an' ma girl-fren. Sometimes yu can be so stupid, ah tired o' messin wif yu.

Irv – Sorry 'bout dat, Roy. Fo' once ah thoat yu were spressin yore true feelin's.

Roy – Yu're OK, Irv, but at times, an' not all day, eber day.

Irv – Ah try to be wa-eber yu want me to be each day o' de week.

Roy – How 'bout dat day yu wanted to be an airplane. Or, dat time yu wa water an' raged down de street in ribbers. Or de time yu thought yu wa a mountain, big at de bottom an' pointed on top?

Irv – Ah lak'd all dat stuff. Too bad *God* refused mah ultimate desires.

Roy – Dat warn't yore *Djarma.*

Irv – Wa?

Roy – Yu dint forget *Djarma,* did yu?

Irv – Ah tink ah kno's de definition o' *Djarma.*

Roy – Wa dat?

Irv – *Djarma* is bein' wa yu tink yu wud be if yu paid more attention to yore breathin', or yore mud-der, or sump-tin' lak dat.

Roy – No! Dat ain' it. *Djarma* is findin' yore tru self.

Irv – Den if ah ain' me, who is ah?

Roy – Yore an utterly lost *Dick-head* floatin' down a too-steep hill wif hu-mun-gous debts an' no home or money.

Irv – Yu got it so far.

Roy – Doan yu wanna do more wif yore life dan bein' a blob o' mountainous stones an' dirt, pointed at top?

Irv – Dat sounded pretty good fo' a wile,

Roy – How 'bout now? Is yu happy wif yore life? Doan yu wanna' be more dan yu ar'?

Irv – Ah wan' money.

Roy – Yu doan get dat wif *Djarma*. Yu get to do wat yu want wif yu're life - demandin' no consequences lak gettin' paid or laid.

Irv – Yu mean ah cud work all week fo' de cement man an' he doan hafta pay me?

Roy – Only if yu love de work, an' de forms yu built fo' de future concrete wall ar' solid an' reliable an' yu can look back on yore days work an' say, *"Ah done a good job"*.

Irv – Den go home, if der wa any, to an empty frigerator, wif no wife, but no money to cook yore food? Wer ar' kids in all dis?

Roy – Havin' *Djarma* ain' easy.

Irv – Ah can see dat. Ah'd haf to hab 2 jobs. One fo' de *Djarma*, an' one to stay alive.

Roy – Let's say, hold out fo' pay fum de *Cement Contractor*.

Irv – Wa if he doan wanna pay?

Roy – Tell him to go screw himself.

Irv – Souns lak ders more to dis *Djarma* ting dan meets de eye-balls.

Roy – Yu cud fine a more *generous contractor*.

Irv – Yu mean fine somebuddy to pay ya, wile yore doin' yore *Djarma?*

Roy – Or forget de *Djarma* bit an' jus' work fo' de money.

Irv – Isn' dat short-sighted?

Roy – Irv, wer yu bin?

Irv – Ah been down to de shed to scrape da fleas off da monkeys.

Roy – Ah dint kno' yu had monkeys.

Irv – Dey ain' mine, dey's *Ralphs*.

Roy – Who's *Ralph?*

Irv – He's one o' ma frens wooo's married wif six kids an' sometimes fo-gets who he is.

Roy – Does he hab *Djarma?*

Irv – Wa?

Roy – Yu din forget *Djarma* already did yu?

Irv – As ah remember, *Djarma* hab negative *complacency* sometimes mistaken wif *desire*.

Roy – Wat's negative *complaaacency?*

Irv – It ain' desire, It's wa yu're sposed to be doin' wif yore life as long as der ain' no *consequences*.

Roy – In dat case yu gotta' hab 2 jobs, de second fo' money to support yore life. Ah thoat yu were de dumb one an' ah wa de smat one. Now, yu're actin' lak de smat one.

Irv – Ah din say ah knew wat ah wa talkin' 'bout. Ah memorized de answers. By de way wa ar' de answers?

Roy – Ah doan kno', tho ah jus' red de rool book.

Irv – Dat means we boff dumb.

Roy – Looks lak it.

Irv – Maybe yu cud reed de book ober again.

Roy – An' waste de power o' me eye-balls? One book's enough.

Irv – Ah's tired o' *Djarma*. Less change de subject.

Roy – Yeah! Wa's more important dan de meaning o' yore life?

Irv – *Blueberry Pie.*

Roy – Ah shud hab kno'n de ultimate o' yore tinkin.

Irv – We better scrapin' de fleas off monkeys.

Roy – Yu say *Ralph* sometimes fo-gets who he is. Do he kno' his name?

Irv – He kno's its *Ralph!* He not dat far gone.

Roy – Do he kno' he's a farmer?

Irv – Most o' de time. Sometimes he tink he's a *former-farmer,* but dat doan work.

Roy – Mus' be hard on de missus.

Irv – She jus' wack him in de gonads an' tell him wa to do!

Roy – Dat does it, OK? Do de kids do wat de parents ask?

Irv – Dey runnin' all ova da place, messin' up de yard, lettin' de animals out, an' creatin' a nightmare fo' de *former-farmer's* wife.

Roy – Mus' be hard on de wife. Wat's she do?

Irv – Drinkin' mostly. She takes a bottle o' wine out unner one o' de remainin' trees an' sits on de swing an' guzzles de booze 'til she passes out an' falls backward out o' de swing upside down onto de groun'.

Roy – Not an enviable life.

Irv – While scrubbin' floors, she dreamed she wa a princess, but dat dint work. She's been suicidal fo' years.

Roy – Souns lak dey both cud use some *Djarma.*

Irv – Ah wish ah could trow some *Djarma* on dem an' dey would suddenly live a normal life, *if wat dey hab is not normal,* but no, dat's wat life tricked out fo' dem an' deys forced to be stuck wif it.

Roy – Do yu wish yu were dem?

Irv - Not on yur life.

Roy – Wa do yu wish fo' dem?

Irv – Peace, love an' *Blueberry Pie*

Ober de Ribber

Irv – Ah love runnin' in de hills. *"Ober de Ribber an' Trew de Woods, to Grand-fadder's House Ah Go."*

Roy – Doan yu tink yu're bein' a little melo-dramatic?

Irv – Wy? Wa ma story too melo? Wa ma story too dramatic?

Roy – Ribber is kinda melo, eben if yu spelled ribber wrong, an' de fack yore runnin' *"Trew de Woods"* could be seen as escapin' life, – tho not really. Ah ask ma-sef wat wa dramatic 'bout dat? Yu're right. *Yu ain' melo or dramatic!*

Irv – Wa wa ah, den?

Roy – A piece o' wanderin' nobody, loose in de rollin' prairies, an' lost in terrifyin' woods.

Irv – Ah disagreeeee! Ah a piece o' humanity scramblin' 'roun da greedy earth tryin' to get a buck.

Roy – Yu mean tryin' to *borrow* a buck. Wer's dat 10 yu owe me?

Irv – Ah tole yu. Yu gonna get it *Saturday*.

Roy – Das wa yu say, but ah neber do.

Irv – OK! Here's de ten!

Roy – Wa? Yu gonna gib me de ten now?

Irv – Ah tired o' yu goin' on an' on 'bout me owin' yu money.

Roy – Now dat yu forcin' yu-sef bein' responsible! How cum yu got money now an' dint hab none in de pass?

Irv – Ah sold sump-tin' important to me.

Roy – Wa dat?

Irv – Ma pet *alligator*.

Roy – Not yore stored in de refrigerator slew o' *Blueberry Pies?*

Irv – Yu tink ah'm *crazy?*

Roy – No! Ah guess not. Yu'd hab to be foamin' at de mouth wif yore eyes waterin' befor yu'd connect wif dat *alligator* milestone.

Irv – Now yu kno' woo ah really am.

Roy – Yeah, habin a pet alligator an' all. How big de *alligator?*

  Irv – He wa 12-feet long an' had razor-sharp teeth dat could bite thru a 4 x 12 wood plank before eatin' it.

Roy – Dat big, huh?

  Irv – He really lak'd razor-back hogs, wich we fed em by de dozen.

Roy – Wa else?

  Irv – One time he tried to eat a donkey.

Roy – Did de donkey complain?

  Irv – He seemed to go along wif it at firs', but den wen de *alligator* snapped at his head it provoked his anger.

Roy – Wa did he do'?

  Irv – He karate-kiked de *alligator* in de libber an' trompled down on his tail.

Roy – Did de *alligator* learn frum dis *in-humane treatment?*

  Irv – *Aligator's* ar' a slow-study. de *alligator* trew up, an' wif a couple o' teeth missin', crawled in de bushes to take a nap.

Roy – Well! Dat shows me a little *alligator* adventure dat wud neber hab crossed ma mind until nap-time. Yu gonna get a new *alligator?*

Irv – Naw! Ah tink ma *alligator* days is obbber. Ah tink ah gonna get a *Polar Bear.*

Roy – Dat doan sound too smart. He might eat yu wen yore sleepin'.

Irv – Yu tink so? Ah cud tie him up real good.

Roy – Tied up *Polar Bears* doan lak to be tied up. Dey might bite thru de ropes, get loose an' mall wa-eber passers-by der ar', wich might be yu.

Irv – Yu tink so?

Roy – It's *a guaranteed truism.*

Irv – Wa dat?

Roy – Wa yu see is wa yu git!

Irv – *"Avy Doovy, Skinnima Doozy, ah love yu cause yu're a Floozy."*

Roy – Is dat all yu got to say? Whooo yu talkin' to? Wy'nt yu tink o' sumtin great, lak *"Our Fathers, who art in Heben – Hallow-Ed be Dye Name."*

Irv – Das de *Lord's Prayer*. Yu a religious person, or wa?

Roy - No! Ah ain' no religious person, more cut fum de *Atheist* mode.

Irv – Wa is yu den?

Roy – Ah's a *Polly-Cracker!*

Irv – No yu ain'! Ah kno' yu too long. Yu ain' no *Polly-Cracker*. Wa is a *Polly-Cracker*, anyway?

Roy – It ain' nuf-fin'. It's jus' sump-tin' un-beknownst flowin' tru' ma haid an' unner ma hair.

Irv – Is dat wa dese conversation's ar' all 'bout? Meaning-less words as *Raucous* sounds: a *promulgated* attack on de ears distributed wif-out corre-shun directly to ma earlobes wif-out a thought to *Gramma?*

Roy – Wa's *raucous* an' *promulgated?*

   Irv – Ah doan kno'. Yu look it up. ah ain' no *dic-shunary.*

Roy – *Raucous* is unpleasantly loud an' *promulgated* means declaring publicly, so yu wa almos' right.

   Irv – Well, ah hope to *Mother-Mercy* ah wa! Ah always did love words, eben iffen ah din kno' wa dey meant.

Roy – Well, yu sure won de *Nobel Prize* on dat one, eben tho de context used wa *ridiculously juvenile.*

   Irv – Yeah? Well, yu're *juvenile* too.

Roy – Ah is not.

   Irv – Not only dat, but yu're an *argument-tive fool.*

Roy – Ah am not!

   Irv – Yu cain't eben say *"Avi doovy, Skinnima Doozy. Ah luv yu cause yure a Floozy."*

Roy – Ah could, but ah doan want to. Das stupid.

Irv – Ah can be both stupid an' ignorant.

Roy – Yu can say dat again.

Irv – Dat would be re-petitive.

Roy – Yu're dat too!

Irv – Ah can be dat too, stupid, ignorant an' competitive.

Roy – Wa 'bout boring?

Irv – Ah'm stupid, ignorant, competitive an' boring.

Roy – Dat 'bout covers it. We've wrapped up de basic dumb-ness o' Irv, an' can get on to bettr tings!

Irv – Wa dat?

Roy – Ah jus' got a job promotion.

Irv – Wa yu goan be doin'.

Roy – Ah'l be designin' de new 2,000 seat theater in *Hollywood* so all de stars can walk up & down de blue carpet to take der awards, in case any cum 'long.

Irv – No shit! Doan yu mean red carpet?

Roy – No! Ah decided to change it fum red to blue 'cause blue means sanity an' red means *"Over de Hill an' Tru de Woods."*

Irv – Wa yu tink it should be?

Roy – *"De horse kno's de way to carry de sleigh trew de soft an' driftin' snow.*

Irv – Yu've got those lyrics rite.

Roy – Wa yu tink o' de news?

Irv – It's goin' to put a neon light on top o' ma girl-fren's haid.

Roy – Is she demonstrative?

Irv – Only while on stage dancin' an' kickin' her legs on high.

Roy – Hey, Irv, yu got a minute?

Irv – Ah got ma haid up ma *Butt* an' ma *Finger on da Trigger o' Love.*

Roy – Wif de *Finger on de Trigger,* ah still doan wan' yu to kill nobody-specially me.

Irv – Is it *Sump-tin' Urgent, Sump-tin' Hot, Sump-tin'* to make me *Drunk, or Doodely Squat?*

Roy –No! It's *Sump-tin' Stupid* an' *Ignorant, Snoring or Boring* – Sump-tin' yu'd tink wa 'specially *Goring?*

Irv – Den no, Ah doan wanna do it.

Roy – Ah gonna gib yu money!

Irv – Now de nine horses ar' humpin' an' jumpin' in front o' de stagecoach ready fo' a tromp unto *Frisco.*

Roy – Ah thought yu'd change yore mind.

Irv – Wa ah spossed to do?

Roy - Change da *Cat-Box-Do.*

  Irv - Ah did dat yestiday.

Roy - It's full again. Ah gotta make a fast trip to
        Tim-Buck-Too an' already kissed ma wife, de
        car is gassed, an' ah'm ready to purr.

  Irv - Ah doan hab no time fo' dat.

Roy - Wa yu mean,

  Irv - Ah writin' a song called *"Ah Doan Kno' Wy
        De Roses Grow."*

Roy - Neider du ah, but dat song already been
        written. Anyway, who cares wy de *Roses
        Grow?*

  Irv - Sum-budy already wrote dat song? When
        dat?

Roy - It wa sung by *Glenn Miller's* band 'round 1942.
        How ol' wa yu at dat time?

  Irv - Ah wa minus-68 years old.

Roy - Dat means yu were born 'bout de turn o' de
        century. An' had de education o' a gnat.

  Irv - Yu won't so smart either. When were yu
        born?

Roy – 1998!

Irv – Das minus-26 years. Yu had de smarts o' a raccoon.

Roy – Ah doubt if ah wa dat smart. De rest o' de song was, *"Money We Really Doan Need. We'll Make Out All Right"* – sung by *Glenn Miller* an' de *Modernaires* an' also on de *Juke Box* eber *Saturday Night.*

Irv – How-ja learn all dat musical historical stuff?

Roy – Usin' de *Internet* fo' brains.

Irv – Ah do dat sometimes. Maybe yu cud get de *Internet* to change yore *Cat-Box-Do.*

Roy – Dat sum kind o' joke, or wa?

Irv - Ah'll gib it dat. Yu cain't ask a piece o' hard-ware to do yore baby-sittin'.

Roy – Wonner if *Al* could change de *Cat-Box-Do.*

Irv – Wy-nt ya let de cat change his own *Cat-Box-Do?*

Roy – He caint do thet. Yu need somebudy wif brains to change de *Cat-Box-Do.*

Irv – Ah got brains enuff.

Roy – Dat's wy ah selected yu fo' de job. Ah knew yu wudn't mess up impotant work.

Irv – Tanks fo' de complement, Roy. Seein' as how somebody already wrote *"Ah Doan Kno' Wy De Roses Grow"*, ah'll take de *Cat-Box-Do* job an' let de *Debil take de Hinemost.*

Roy – Ah knew ah could depen' on yu.

Irv – Ah'l leave dat *Cat-Box-Do* sparklin' clean as if in storage o' polished stainless steel brain surgical operational instruments designated fo de cut-open brain.

Roy – It doan hab to be dat good, de *Cat-Box-Do* holds stinky effluents frum nuttin less dan a cat.

Irv – Yu cant be too clean.

Roy – Wa horrible an' obnoxious mind-bendin', oblivious, dis-array yu got to tell me today?

Irv – De collapse o' de *North Abenue Bridge* into de *Chicago Ribber*, an' de drownin' o' un-countable people, wif de loss o' cars an' trucks, an' streetcars, an' trains, dat might *Call Yu're Bluff.*

Roy – Effen its true, dat wooda blown ma mind to bonkers an' back.

Irv – Heck, no, Roy, it's not true. It's a fig-ment o' *ma imagination.*

Roy – Ah dint kno' yore mind wa filled wif figs, tho cumin frum yu, ah see de possibility.

Irv – Wa do yu really wan' frum me?

Roy – Answer de question, as if a flock o' dem birds flew over de *Foo-Ball* game.

Irv – Wich one? *De Sunday Game* or de *Saturday Game?*

Roy – Ah doan kno', maybe de *Tuesday Game.*

Irv – Dere warn't no *Tuesday Game*.

Roy – How do yu kno'?

Irv – Cum to tink o' it, ah doan kno' de schedule o' *Foo-Ball* Games. In fack, ah doan eben lak *Foo-Ball*.

Roy – Wa? Yu male an' doan lak *Foo-Ball?* Ebery-Budy das male lak's *Foo-Ball*.

Irv – Yu mean, since ah doan lak *Foo-Ball* ah'm not *Male?* So, wa am ah?

Roy – Yu *Male* an' doan lak *Foo-Ball* jus lak *Women* woo doan lak it either.

Irv – OK! Ah'll change ma preferences so ah wone be *Female*.

Roy – Yu'd do dat jus' to prove yu're *Male?*

Irv – Wa better reason?

Roy - *Integrity? Troooth-fulness*. Being *Honest*. Habin' strong *Moral Principals?*

Irv – Yu tink ah doan hab no strong *Moral Principals?*

Roy – Perhaps one or two.

Irv – Wud yu believe ah doan lak *Bask-R-Ball*, or *Soccer*, or *Tennis*, or *Hockey*, or how far yu can trow a *Tomato*.

Roy – Dey doan hab no *Trowin' Tomato* sports.

Irv – How 'bout Trowin a *Golf-Ball?*

Roy – Dey doan trow *Golf-Balls*. Dey play a game based on how many swings an' hits yu doan make, wins de game.

Irv – Yu mean takin' de most swings doan win de game?

Roy – De game be called *Golf.*

Irv – Now yu can see wy ah doan lak sports.

Roy – Ah'm tinkin' o' yu differently.

Irv – How so?

Roy – Yu're softer, more sensitive, more poetic. Someone woo laks *improve-isational dance.*

Irv – Das it! Ah lak *"Hang Yur Haid Ober, Hear de Wind Blow, Look at de Skyline, Soon it will Snow".*

Roy – Das it! Yu hab a poetic frame o' mine!

Irv – *"Down in da valley, de valley so low. Hang yur haid ober, hear de win' blow".*

Roy – Das enough. Irv. We got de point. No need to push it, once ah kno' woo yu ar'.

Irv – *"Hang yore haid ober, hear de win' blow. Down in de Valley, de Valley so low - ".*

Roy – Yeah! We get it. We kno'. *"Hang yore head ober, hear de win' blow."*

Irv – Doan yu wan' kno' woo ah am?

Roy – No! Das enuff!

Purple Eye 36

Roy – Irv, wa-cha got fo' me today? Ah hope it's not 'bout yore mudder-in-law *Pressin' De-Pedal-to-da-Medal* an' runnin' headlong into an on-cummin' truck wif her wrinkled bonnet bein' blown off her haid an' run over in a tangled mess by a modor-cycle.

Irv – Das pretty close. It wa her stocking. She ripped a full-length stocking frum thighs to feet dat were filled wif slimy mud sqeezin' between her toes an' forcin' her to take a bath.

Roy - Wich leg?

Irv – One or de *Udder*. Ah doan kno'. Doan hang me! Ah doan care wich leg, anyway.

Roy – Wa she runnin' fum a car, or wa she upset 'bout sump-tin' her son did at school lak de rank insultation o' a school teacher, or wa?

Irv – Her son didn' do nuttin, he wa bein' kept after school fo' pullin' a classmates hair. He ripped half o' it off an' she fell down an' bit his ankle rippin' his sock.

Roy – Wa de girl kep' after school?

  Irv – Yeah! She got three wollops on de bottom wif a paddle an' had to do 33 push-ups.

Roy – Boy! Dey sure ar' strict.

  Irv – Ah wouldn' wanna get caught.

Roy – Wy wa de wife whoo got hit by de modorcycle upset?

  Irv – She foun' out her husband wa *Trinkin'-to-Dinkin'* anoder woman.

Roy – Wa she right, or makin' de hole ting up?

  Irv – She doan kno'. Her husband had anod-der story, wich she also dint believe.

Roy – Wa wa it?

  Irv – He said he wa hitch-hiken an' dis strange, but good-lookin' girl picked him up an' drove him to her house wer' we doan kno' if der wa any real fryin' o' eggs or gobblin o' dem down - as if der's no yest'day.

Roy – Heck! *Das jus' in-substantial evidence.* Wa do he say?

Irv – He say he's as innocent as *5-year-old* bein' accused o' kicken a cat wile eatin' at its food dish.

Roy – Yu believe dat?

Irv – Ah'l believe anyting dat gets me home in time to eat *Blueberry Pie.*

Roy – Der we go, again. Yu is a *Monster* wen it cums to *Blueberry Pie.*

Irv – Ah do hab ma favorites.

Roy – How 'bout *Apple Pie?*

Irv – Naw! Ah doan lak *Apple Pie.*

Roy – Wa 'bout *Squirrel Pie?*

Irv – Dey doan make *Squirrel Pie.*

Roy – If dey made *Squirrel Pie*, wud yu eat it?

Irv – Ah'd giv' it a shot.

Roy – Da's disgustin'!

Irv – Wy yu ask all dese dum questions?

Roy – Less change de subject. Woo yu takin' to de *New Years Eve* show?

Irv – Wen's dat?

Roy – Nex' year – on *New Years Eve.*

Irv – Ah doan kno'. Dat too far in advance.

Roy – Yu gonna take *Georgia?*

Irv – *Georgia* give me de *Purple Eye!*

Roy – Wa a *Purple Eye?*

Irv – A *Purple Eye* is giben by de one not tellin' de truth.

Roy – *Georgia* ben giben yu de *Purple Eye?*

Irv – Ah doan lak *Georgia* an' de *Purple Eye.* Yu Lak *Purple Eye?*

Roy – Ah neber heard o' no *Purple Eye.*

Irv – Wen *Georgia* looks at yu, yu'll kno'.

Roy – Will it be lak bein' smashed on de noggin wif a heavy club?

Irv – Yeah! An' yu fall face-down on de grass.

Wat Yooo Tink? 37

Roy – Wa yooo tink 'bout de plight o' de worl?

   Irv – Yu mean worl' – wif a *"D"?"*

Roy – Yeah! Ah guess so.

   Irv – Yu doan really care, do yu?

Roy – Yeah! Ah tink ah do.

   Irv – Wy?

Roy – 'Cause dats de place wer we live. If de worl' wern't here, wer ah go?

   Irv – *Gramma's House?*

Roy – Das ridiculous!

   Irv – Den we'd jus' be in someone's imagination.

Roy – If der ain' no someone, der, ain' no imagination.

   Irv – Yu mean if der were no worl' an' no *Grandma's House*, we wudn be der. Wer we be?

Roy – Somewer' else, or more lak'ly, no-wer'.

Irv – Is no-wer wer yu go wen yu die?

Roy – If yu eber were alive, some say wen yu die, yu lib for-eber.

Irv – Yu believe dat?

Roy – No! Only dat wen ah die, ah'll still be in de used-up part o' de *Universe*.

Irv – Kinda lak in de *Uni-berse's* junk pile. Woo will hab used me up?

Roy – Yu used yur-sef up.

Irv – Can we play another game?

Roy – Dat's all she wrote.

Irv – Yu mean ah'm stuck wif ma-sef an' cain't get off?

Roy – Dat's one way to look at it.

Irv – Is'n der anodder way?

Roy – Yu cud claim yore goin' to *Heben,* den ebery-ting's OK.

Irv – Wa's in *Heben?*

Roy – All dose yu luv, dose not special, but made de cut, foreigners, an' people yu neber heard o'.

Irv – Will guys lak *Jeffrey Dahmmer* be der?

Roy – In *Heben* all de bad guys doan make de cut.

Irv – Will ma dead *Mudder-in-Law* be der?

Roy – Probably. Yu may not hab lak'd her, but she didn' piss *God* off enuff to not make de cut.

Irv – Ah wish she weren't der.

Roy – Tough bananas. Yu doan get eberyting yu lak in life.

Irv – Yu goin' to *Heben?*

Roy – Ah spec so. Ah been OK so far, but ah ain' de judge.

Irv – Woo de judge?

Roy - *God*, silly!

Irv – Do dey hab debates?

Roy – No! *God's* word is de law.

Irv – No court o' appeal?

Roy – Yore *Mudder-in-Law* wud be de firs' to appear.

Irv – No way out o' it, eh?

Roy – Ah suppose yu cud form a committee for *Open-Minded Discussions.*

Irv – How yu tink dat wud go?

Roy – Ah doan tink, ah'd bet ma *Final Buck* on it.

Irv – Maybe we cud slip sumebudy an extra *Sawbuck* to *Slant-de-Vote.*

Roy – An put one over on *God?* Ah doan tink so.

Irv – Cum to tink o' it, ma *Mudder-in-Law's* not dat bad.

An'-a-Half 38

Irv – Ah just got bak frum ice skatin' class wer we learned to do a re-berse doubel *twister-an-a-half,* or so.

Roy – Wa yu mean *"or so."* Seems lak yu eider wer' or wer' not to do de *twister-an-a-half.*

Irv – He said if we cudn't do de *"an'-a-half-twister"* it wud be *OK* an' we wudn be kicked out o' class.

Roy – Yu mean in some classes if yu caint do de *"an-a-half-twister,"* yu're kicked out o' class?

Irv – Ah doan kno' 'bout udder classes, ah jus' kno' 'bout mine.

Roy – Yu doan hab to get huffy 'bout it.

Irv – Ah ain' huffy, ah jus' get ticked off cause yu criticize eber-ting ah do.

Roy – Sorry 'bout it. Yu gettin' disturbed a lot lately. Sump-tin else botherin' yu?

Irv – Yeah! *Gladys* woan let me cum ober to her house.

Roy – Wy's dat'?

  Irv – She says ah smell lak unwashed socks an' doesn' lak it when ah pick ma nose or *Fart*.

Roy – Ah can see her point. Yu do smell funny an' yu ar' always pickin' yore nose an' *Fartin'*.

  Irv – She says ah shud jump inside de laundry machine wile its goin' an' stay in der fo' an *hour-an-a-half*.

Roy – De *Apple* doan fall far fum de *Palooza*.

  Irv – Das a funny *Aphorism*.

Roy – Wa's de meaning o' *Affor-issms?*

  Irv – Ah thoat yu wer' de smart one, an' here ah am re-splaining to yu de meanin' o' de word *"Aphorism."*

Roy – OK! So, doan tell me wa it is.

  Irv – An *aphorism* is a pithy statement offering an opinion.

Roy – Lak wa?

  Irv – *"Doan take any Wooden Nickels."*

Roy – Ah'm not gonna do dat.

Irv – Dat's wat de *Aphorism* says.

Roy – Wa do de *Aphorism* say?

Irv – If de *Wooden Nickel* is made outa wood, it won't buy nuf-fin.

Roy – Wa if it's painted silver an' looked jus' lak a *Nickel?*

Irv – If it ain' made o' wa-eber dey make *Nickel's* out o', it won't buy nuf-fin.

Roy – OK! If it ain' made outa wa-eber a *Nickel's* made o', it ain' no *Nickel.*

Irv – Das rite! Dat answer is flyin' on top o' yore minds flagpole an' is a visual *Olympic* winner.

Roy – Boy, Irv, dis time yu sure put de chair under ma bottom jus' before ah sat down.

Irv – Glad to be o' service. Any-ting else ah can hep yu wif?

Roy – Yeah! Yu cud tell me de differnce between a *Horse* an' a *Donkey.*

Irv – Das an easy one. Yu get on de *Horse* an' say

giddy-yap an' yu go fo' a ride. Yu get on de *Donkey* an' say giddy-yap an' de *Donkey* doan move.

Roy – Wy not?

Irv – Ah doan kno', but dat's how yu tell de dif-fernce.

Roy – Ah doan tink ah gotta kno' dat bad.

Irv – Anyting else yu need to kno', or wa to do, or wer to go, or tings to buy, or brains yore missin'?

Roy – No! Ah now kno' ebery-ting ah need to kno' to keep me functionin' at ma normally unaware state o' mind.

Irv – Glad to hab been o' service. Good to hab yu as a continuing companion strugglin' thru our uneasy tromp tru life.

Buck-Tim-Two 39

Irv – Jus' got bac' frum *Buck-Tim-Two* an' boy wa da wed-dr *mercurial.*

Roy – Wa *mercurial?*

Irv - A *mercurial* person is changeable or unpredictable, but in dis case it means de wether is changeable an' unpredictable. Does dat untangle yore *bugs-feet* frum yore spider-web?

Roy – Ah wone't talkin' 'bout untanglin' *bugs-feet* frum spider-webs.

Irv - Wa wa yu talkin' 'bout'?

Roy – Nothin'! Yu brought up *Buck-Tim-Two.* Ah tought yu meant *Tim-Buck-Two.* Did yu mean dat?

Irv – Nope! *Buck-Tim-Two* is somewer' in de *Northwest* part o' da *Seben-Lost-Forests* in *Nebraska.*

Roy – Der's *Seben*, huh? How many d'yu tink der wer'?

Irv – Doan kno'! Wa jus' catchin' snakes an'

puttin' em in a trailer.

Roy – How many dja get?

  Irv – Fourteen.

Roy – Wa dja do wif em?

  Irv – Tru dem in de ribber.

Roy – Drowned dem eh?

  Irv – No! Dey water snakes an' swam away, free!

Roy – Wy ja do dat'?

  Irv – Cause we're free wif our love o' animals an' snakes an' its de human ting to do. We're not no reptiles.

Roy – Den wy doan yu jus' stay home?

  Irv – Yeah! Gess we shud hab.

Roy – Woo went wif yu?

  Irv – *Gretta* an' her girl-fren *Mabel.*

Roy – Did dey hab a good time?

  Irv – *Gretta* broke her thumb-nail an' *Mabel* stubbed her toe.

Roy – An ah gess yu com-forted dem?

Irv – No! Ah fell down on ma side an' rolled 50-feet down de slope endin' up floatin' upside down in waste-water-deep water wif *Piranhas* sizen me up fo' brekfast.

Roy – Dat must hab ben de cat's meow sung at night, heard all over *Nebraska,* an' threatened by *Piranhas.*

Irv – It weren't dat good!

Roy – Course yu changed clothes an' enjoyed bein' *dry as a willow-wisp* til morning.

Irv – If only? Ah din hab extra clothes, ah jus' sat in de sun fo' a couple o' hours an' played *Tiddly-Winks* wif de girls til dinner time.

Roy – Woo won de *Tiddly-Winks* game?

Irv – Gretta won de first, third an' fourteeth games by huge margins, but lost to Mabel woo won de second an' fourth to thirteenth games by skimpy margins.

Roy – Dju win any?

Irv – Nope! Mostly cause ah sprained ma thumb.

Roy – Ah can see playin' *Tiddly-Winks* wud be mighty

stressful on yore thumb. Dju get home all right?

Irv – We drove home by night thru a hevy rainstorm wif lightnin' dat bounced off our roof onto a power pole dat crashed down settin' 14 acres an' 2 houses in a field o' fire.

Roy – Wa yu OK?

Irv – We wa fine until it began to hail - poundin' de roof an' breakin' our windshield wif water gettin' all over ma tuxedo-suit.

Roy – Dat mus' o' been tuff.

Irv – Den a *torfoon* leaped outa de sky an began swirlin' an' spinnen' an' twistin' in front o' us lookin' lak it gonna' pick us up an trow us outa de *Nebraska Ball Park.*

Roy – Dat soun' really hair-raisin', rain, hit by lightning, struck by a *torfooon* an' all. Wa did de girls say?

Irv – Dey slepp thru it.

Erudite 40

Roy – Ah gotta get goin' to meet ma girl-fren, *Gladys*.

Irv – Wy? She gettin' off at da station in 15-minutes, an' yu gotta pick er up wif 'er dog, *Cauliflower?*

Roy – Yeah! No! Her dog's name is *Salami*. Las' week he wa mistak'n fo' a san-wich wif 2 pieces o' beef wif minimally inladen *Tabasco-Buttered Da-Da.*

Irv – Good ting dey noticed jus' in time dat he wa a dog.

Roy – De dog wa *ecstatic*.

Irv – Wa *ecstatic?*

Roy – *Ecstatic* means happy or excited.

Irv – Tank yu fo' bein' so *Erudite.*

Roy – Wa *Erudite?*

Irv – *Erudite* means great kno'ledge, learned or scholarly.

Roy – Ah cud hab *In-ferred* dat!

  Irv – Wa *In-ferred?*

Roy – *In-ferred* means to make a *well-informed gess.*

  Irv – Yu sure ar' dum.

Roy – Yu ain' so smat yur-sef.

  Irv – Wadda yu gon to do wif *Gladys?*

Roy – She gonna take me *ice-skatin'.*

  Irv – Yu kno' how to ice-skate?

Roy – Learned it watchin' movies.

  Irv - Doan tink dat wud help much.

Roy – Probably not, ah'm jus' makin' luv wif *Gladys* in ma spare time.

  Irv – Der's *Gladys* now! Hi, *Gladys!*

Gladys – Ah done believe ah kno' yu.

Roy – Irv, dis is *Gladys. Gladys,* dis is Irv.

Gladys – Glada meetcha Irv, Hope de debil hab

stayed away fum yore wide-open door.

Irv – Wa?

Roy – *Gladys* wa jus' makin' a *Homily*.

Irv – Wa a *Homily?*

Roy – A *Homily* is a *Sermon* or *Religious Topic.*

Irv – Ar' we in *church?*

Roy – In *Gladys's* mine, we is always in *church.*

Irv – Is she a *Religious Nut?*

Roy - Jus' lookin' at her, yu'd neber kno', but in reality, she's *IS* a *Religious Nut*, an' da's *No Secret.*

Irv – How cum yu goin' out wif her?

Roy – Ah doan kno'. She not lak ma usual *Perseption's.*

Irv – Wa *Perseption's?*

Roy – *Perseption's* is *Cognition* or *Understandin'.*

Irv – Dis too difficult fo' me. Ah quit!

Roy – Yu cain't quit. Yu in life. Yu gonna quit life?

Yu suicidal, or wa?

Irv – No! Ah ain' suicidal. Ah jus' doan unner-stan.

Roy – *Gladys!* Wa yu got to say 'bout dis *Pre-dicam-dent.*

Gladys – Wa a *Pre-dicament?*

Roy – Not yu too! Ah tought yu wa smart an' now yu show me yu is jus' as dum as *Irv.*

Gladys – Wa *Pre-dicament?*

Roy – *Pre-dicament* is *Unpleasant* or *Embarrassin' Situation.*

Gladys – Lak Ah doan hab no money fo' de *train-ride?*

Roy – Yu done hab money fo' ar' *train-ride?*

Gladys – No! Ah done believe ah do. Do yu hab money fo' de *train-ride?*

Roy – No! Ah done hab no money fo' de *train-ride.*

Gladys – Less go by car.

Outer Space 41

Roy - Yu eber hear 'bout *outer space?*

  Irv - No, Roy, ah neber herd 'bout no *outer space.* Wa's dat?

Roy - Schnott 'bout *inner space.*

  Irv - Heck! Ah knu dat wen yu said *inner space* stead o' *outer space.*

Roy - We is all-reddy *IN inner space.*

  Irv – Ah woont be *any-wer else.*

Roy - Dey's crazy tings goin' on in *outer space.*

  Irv - Wer *IS* outer space?

Roy - Yu kno' wer de moon is?

Irv - Yep! In de night sky.

Roy - Yu smarter dan ah thoat. De moon ib in *outer space.*

Irv - *Hooooo-eeee!*

Roy - No! Der's more. Dey funny tings floatin' 'roun up in *outer space,* so fas' money cain't buy a *dood-dell-ley, ding-dong, or a wibb-belly-wa-wa.*

 Irv - We cain't? Do dey get *ar-rested?*

Roy - Der ain' no *police-men* in no *outer space.*

 Irv - How fast dey go?

Roy - *Whim-wham-tank-yu-mam-ahm-so-hungry gonna eat-a-ham. (san-wich, dat is.)*

 Irv - Kin ah go too?

Roy - Yu chase em in yo fighter-jet, dey zoom dis-way, dat-way, dive in de ocean, come out, split in two, an' disappear *ober de sea an' tru' de woods,* gone in a blink.

 Irv - Can we catch em an' ask em wy dey do dat?

Roy - Dey will not let us catch em. Dey escape goin' faster dan de speed o' light.

 Irv - How fast dat?

Roy - One hunderd eighty-six thousan' miles per second, faster dan de crow flies. About *1.25 seconds to de moon.*

Irv - Das faster dan catchin' a late bus.

Roy - Luukin lak a banana, sump-times dey cum inna group o' ten, 3 o' dem disa-pear, den 5 cum back an' go out.

Irv - Wa yu mean, *dey go out?*

Roy - Wen *dey go out,* dey *diss-a-peeer.*

Irv - *Well, whoop-de-dooo!*

Roy - Das *in-cred-i-bobble!*

Irv - Dat blows ma whole card.

Roy - Dat knocks me off ma *pedestal,* if ah wa eber on a *pedestal.*

Irv - Yu ain' on no *pedestal.*

Roy - Ah tinks ah is. Some cum inna a glass *sphere* de size o' a basket-ball wif a cube inside wif four corners touching de internal glass an' glowin' lak a *meat-ball.*

Irv - Wa fo'?

Roy - No-buddy kno's wa fo', dey jus' do.

Irv - Done, dat blow ma *hanky-dank?* Whooda thoat-it? Eben ma wa-dya-call-it wa's sum-wat peeky-eyed.

Roy - Obviously, not yu. Wa de author say, is dey gonna treat *grab-i-diddy* lak soun' an' light as ib it were a wave an' enclosed in a ball?

  Irv - Wy dey do dat?

Roy - Den dey go *Hanky-Panky-Zanky-Danky-Poo-Poo,* wave dey arms, trow a match off a hunderd story buildin' an sit on a frog fo' fouty-five minutes.

  Irv - Wy dey do dat?

Roy - It's sump-tin else to do.

  Irv - Dat gonna work?

Roy - Prob-bly not.

  Irv - Ah gotta few ideas 'long dat line.

Roy - Wa da?

  Irv - Ah fo-get.

⸕⸜⸝⸞

Liddle Trip 42

Irv - Hey, Roy, ahma tinkin ah wanna go onna liddle trip.

Roy - Yeah! Wer yu wanna go?

Irv - Sum-place wer de sun doan shine, always mine, easy to fine, pleasure to dine, address wif nine, re-laxin' kine, dat rhyme wif pine,

Roy - Yu's a poet an' doan kno' it. Yu hab a tickle-lish project. De sun doan shine on de back o' de moon.

Irv - It do too! We jus' cain't see it cause de back o' de moon only facin' space, not us.

Roy - Wa?

Irv - Yu sposs-ed to kno' dat.

Roy - Ah do? Less see? Yeah! Now ah see it connectin' in ma brain lak a concete block trown into a puddle o' wet cement.

Irv - An *astronaut* visited de back side o' de moon? Wa his name?

Roy - De *Inter-net* say, *Frank Borman, Jim Lovell,* an' *William Anders* saw it *69-miles up in space.* Eeech moon-day, boff sides o' de moon sees de sun.

Irv - Yu goin too fas' fo' ma brain to take in de *con-fab-u-la-shuns.* Abba doan-a kno' wa dat means.

Roy - Den forget it. De *info-ma-shun* ib not nece-sary fo' yo *no-brain* to kno' - no-how, no-place, no-wer.

Irv - All *info-ma-shun* ib *nec-cess-sary* fo' de carryin'-on o' *life-bunky.*

Roy - How yu kno' dat?

Irv - Ah red it sump-twer's in a book called *Knowledge fo' de Wimper-Dink.*

Roy - Ah all-reddy read dat book.

Irv - How wa it?

Roy - OK! If yu wer' a *Winper-Dink.*

Irv - Ah still wanna go onna liddle trip to *sum-place* wer de sun doan shine.

Roy - Take a buncha naps, yu'll get ober it.

Irv - Das trowin it away. Doan yu wanna see de *satis-fack-shun* in ma 'hole *organ-a-mistic uni-fi-ca-shun?*

Roy - Wa?

Irv - Doan yu wanna get jus' a glimpse o' de solid center o' ma *hart's desire-bunky?*

Roy - No! Ahm OK wif it.

Irv - Doan yu wanna' get *habbie-de-scrabbies* unner yo belt-buck-ell fum jus' de thoat o' me cummin to ma wild-ess *imag-i-na-shee-un?*

Roy - No! Ahm OK wif it.

Irv - Den yu a *mon-ster.*

Roy - Ahm jus' *pract-i-cal.* Yu neber gonna fine no place to go wif shine, mine, fine, dine, nine, rhymes wif pine, in it.

Irv - Ah kin look, cain't ah?

Roy - Wait a-minut'. *Ah kno's Sum-place to go wer de sun doan go,* packed wif dough, eaten by foe, owned by Joe, brain-power low, cain't eben row, waitin' fo' a tow.

Irv - Hey! Das pretty guud! Hooo-ray fo' yu! *Gobble-de-goo-goo, ding-dash-doo-doo!*

Roy - Shall we put dat liddle tiger to beddy-by?

Irv - Ah still wanna go on a liddle trip wer de sun doan shine or sun doan show. How do ah get der?

Roy – Take a bus.

Irv – Bus-driber kno' how to get der?

Roy - Wer *IS* de sun doan shine, always mine, easy to fine, ding-dong, rhyme-rhyme?

Irv – Ahmma notta kno'.

Roy - Looks lak yu crossin' de ocean wif-out no sails or motor or oars. Kinda lak waitin' fo' a hurricane.

Irv - If ah may, ahl fine a way, to eat a liddle hay, cause ah jus' wanna say ah collects a liddle pay dat sparks a liddle ray to fine a proper way to while-away da day.

Roy - Yu is a poet, an' still don't kno' it.

Roy - Hey, Irv, ah bin readin' 'bout aliens fum outer space.

 Irv - Yu wanta medal, or sump-tin?

Roy - Jus' thoat yu'd lak to hear 'bout travels tru galaxies, suns, plan-ets, moons, stars, asteroids, com-ets, star-dust, time, space an' udder ting-bunkies o' dat *Ka-leeber.*

 Irv - Wer *IS* outer space?

Roy - *S-schnot* in inner space.

 Irv - Ah cud o' *sur-mised* dat.

Roy - Wa *sur-mised?*

 Irv - *An educated guess.*

Roy - Can ah get on wif ma carrion-ons?

 Irv - Wa fo' yu got to *elaborate?*

Roy - Wa's *elaborate?*

 Irv - *Gib details.* Cud yu please tell me 'bout inner.

outer space, or sum kinda space o' wich ah
neber herd o'?

Roy - De book say, aliens surround der spaceship wif
a ball o' energy made fum de wave-lenth o'
Earth's grab-i-diddy.

Irv - Wy dey do dat?

Roy - Wif de space ship inside de ball o' grab-i-diddy
dey can zip answers to space faster dan de
speed o' lite.

Irv - How fas' dey go?

Roy - Dey wip here an' der faster dan eatin' *blueberry pie.*

Irv - Ah lak *blue-berry pie.*

Roy - Yu'd seem like de nuclear bomb energy wud
re-splode away into de icy space o' de un-
known, so dey mus' convert it to sumptin lak
anti-grab-i-diddy to increase pressure makin'
de ball stick to de flyin' disc wile zoomin' dis
way an' dat.

Irv - Yu kno dis fo' sure?

Roy - Dis all *spec-u-la-za-shun* on ma part an' hab
ab-so-lute-ly nuffin to do wif *reali-ti-diddy.*

Irv - Yu mean dis story all *horse-shit?*

Roy - Well, ah wudden be so *ex-pli-cit* 'bout it, but yes, it's all *horse-shit.* If Kaku, Tyson an' Joval Harari doan kno, how'm ah spos-sed to kno?

Irv - Wa's *ex-pli-cit?*

Roy - *Ex-pli-cit* means *clearly expres-sed.* Den if de aliens is sub-jeck to hebby pressure fum de ball, in order to lib, dey need a lower pressure inside der disk-lak space-ship.

Irv - Well, la, de da!

Roy - De disk-lak space ships flyin' *INSIDE* de hebby anti-grabi-diddy ball hab a lower intensity to *ac-com-o-ate* de aliens.

Irv - Hoooo-eee! Ma brain am *ober-work'd.* Ah reddy to sit down an' gulp down a ice cream cone - chocolate, if ah may.

Roy - So, dis is wy we cain't sit across de table wif a beer an' say howdy to de aliens fum outer space.

Irv - Wy dat?

Roy - We all die.

Irv - Wy we die?

Roy - We cain't stan' de pressures o' de alien's normal *en-vir-on-ment.*

Irv - Ah jus' hit de curb an' fell off ma roller skates.

Roy - Dat bad, eh?

Irv - Yu've upset ma hole day an' ah need mine-control. Dis too deep fo' mah lak o' brain. Ah neber wan' to blab 'bout de horse-shit agin' o' alien's fum outer space.

Roy - Ah not done yet.

Irv - Less do sump-tin else.

Roy - Wa we gonna do instead.

Irv - Ah thoat we'd take a boat to Madagaskar an' buy a slub o' *Ring-Tailed-Lemurs* an' sell em at da market.

Roy - Das a bad idea.

Irv - Wy dat?

Roy - Yu doan hab no money.

⁂

Mathematics 44

Irv - One, two, three, four, six, seven ...

Roy - *Wait! Wait! Wait!*

Irv - Wa'd ah do now?

Roy - Yu left out five.

Irv - Ah did *not!*

Roy - Yu left out *five.* Doan yu listen to yo-sef wen yu talkin'?

Irv - Ah listen's to ma-sef!

Roy - Den wy yu not pickin' up da missin' *five?*

Irv - Ah made a *re-cordin'* o' ma-sef fo' de speech ah *sup-poossed* to gib on *Friday.*

Roy - Well, den, play de *re-cordin'.*

Irv - *(Plays tape.)* One, two, three, four, six... *Oh yeah.*

Roy - Wa yu got to say fo' yo-sef?

Irv - Sorry ah be a *dum-ass*.

Roy - Das all yu got to say?

Irv - No-buddies *perfeck*. Even yu ain' *perfeck*. Ah'm *perfeck* as a *spider web*.

Roy - Is *spider webs perfeck?*

Irv - Ah neber seen a bad one.

Roy - Wa hab a *spider web* got to do wif yo *speech?*

Irv - Yu missed de *five,* a key part o' yo countin' *speech.*

Roy - *Re-splainin* how to count 'rong makes sense, but ah tinks eva-buddy all-reddy knows how to count *'rong.*

Irv - How ah goin' to *re-splain* to de audience how to count *'rong?*

Roy - Yu kno' how to count *'rong?*

Irv - Ah cud count *'rong* eben wif a gun to ma *haid.*

Roy - Well, ah ain' got no gun, but less hear yu count *'rong.*

Irv - Das easy, two, twelve, thirteen, seven, eleven, six...

Roy - As *math-e-ma-tics teacher o' de year,* ah'd say yu be a nat-ural talent fo' countin' *'rong.*

Irv - Tanks fo' de *com-plement.* Kin yu also count *rite?*

Roy - Sure! Easy! Try me out.

Irv - OK! Count *rite.*

Roy - Seven, eight, nine, ten, eleven, twelve, thirteen, an' so on ...

Irv - Das pretty guuud. Ah hear-by gib's yu an "A" fo' *co-opera-shun, spirit* an' *ded-i-ka-shun* to *spider-webs* an' *math-em-matics.*

Roy - Ah do not de-serb such high *comp-i-ments,* but ah do wish yu had more pres-teeege.

Irv - Ah workin' on it.

Roy - Wa's de nex' *sub-jeck* yu gonna teach?

Irv - Tinkin 'bout de alpha-*BET. NOT* 'bout *gamb-lin'.*

Roy - Yu' mean dat *A-B-C* ting? How dat go?

Irv - M is fo' de *Million* tings yu gabe me. *O* is fo' de *Odder* tings yu gabe to me. *T* is fo' de

Trillion tings yu gabe to me, *H* is fo' de *Heck-off-a-lot* of tings yu gabe to me, *E* is fo'...

Roy - *Yeah! Yeah!* Ah get it. Das a take-off on de song called *Mother* written by *Henry Burr* in 1915 an' sung in the 20's & 30's sump-times by *Al Jolson.*

Irv - Stop showin' off yo *not-so-bril-liant mine.* *(mind)*

Roy - It's better-n yores.

Irv - Only fum de stan-poin o' *intel-li-gence.*

Roy - An' spiders.

Irv - Ah'l gib yu dat.

Obsolete 45

Irv - Ma granpa says ah's *obsolete.*

Roy - *Wa's ob-so-lete?*

Irv - *Obsolete* means no longer useful, out- dated,
pie too moldy to eat.

Roy - If a *starbin-to-deff* monkey foun' a *choca-
late cookie* trown away in de alley wif goo-goo
all ober de bottom, yu grandpa ib rite, he'd say
life's too short an' walk away.

Irv - There-fore, boff de monkey an' ah ar'
ob-solete.

Roy - Dat means yu-re boff no longer useful, out-
dated an' *too moldy to eat.*

Irv - My *grandpa* all-readdy tole me dat.

Roy - Wabba yuubba gonna doooba 'bout dat?

Irv - De usual.

Roy - Wa de usual?

Irv - Nuf-fin'.

Roy - Yu cain't do no nuf-fin'. Yu human, eben if yu doan lak it, ebery mornin' yu gotta get up wif fire in yo eyes an' *Go! Go! Go!*

Irv - Ah done wanna do dat.

Roy - *No-buddy* wan' to.

Irv - Wy dey do it den?

Roy - To stay alibe.

Irv - Ah jus' wanna *sleep, sleep, sleep.*

Roy - If yu gonna do dat, yu gonna *die, die, die.* Yu wanna *die, die, die,* do yu?

Irv - Ah wanna *lib, lib, lib.*

Roy - Den yu gotta *work, work, work.*

Irv - Wa ah gonna work *AT?*

Roy - Yu hafta decide dat fo' yo-sef. Yu needs *Dharma.*

Irv - Wa's *Dharma?*

Roy - *Dharma* is de main purpose o' yore life.

Irv - Wa dat?

Roy - Dat fo' *YU* to decide.

    Irv - Ah cud bag droppin's fum a *horse* farm an' fro dem away.

Roy - Yu got any *horses?*

    Irv - No.

Roy - Den yu hab to get *horses* drop-pin' tings fo' yu, or fine sump-tin else to do.

    Irv - Ah cud *mop de floors*, or *sweep de kitchen*, or *count de daisys*.

Roy - Dey not gonna pay yu fo' countin' no *daisys*.

    Irv - Dat job *obsolete*, eh?

Roy - Yu hab to pick sump-tin yu proud to do, sump-tin' wer yu can say, *ah did dis,* sump-tin' to make yore *mudder proud as a loud-cloud-inna-crowd.*

    Irv - Ah cud wash dishes, make de' beds, sweep de' libbin-room floor an' mow de lawn an' fix de' roof.

Roy - Now yu talkin'. Pick sump-tin' useful dat bene-fits society an' helps people get along wif dem-selves.

Irv - Ah gonna be a famous photo-grapher takin' pictures o' snows an' rain-storms, an hurricanes an' earth-quaks an' floods an' cloudy-lookin' wa-da-ya-call-its threat-enin de worl an' gramma.

Roy - Dat's pretty, but ah done tink yu gonna make any money *shooootin* dose kind o' pic-shures.

Irv - Wy not? Dey's pretty. Deys de essence o' life, deys de *Dharma* o' de worl', dey's de greates' ting-bunky in da *Uni-berse*.

Roy - People all-reddy kno' 'bout wether. Dey ain gonna pay no money cause dey hab to stay home cause it's rainin'.

Irv - *Wabba, Ahbba, gommba, doooo-ba, now, Roy?*

Roy - Photograph de bad stuff lak one-half o' de cummin election.

Irv - Wich half?

Roy - De ugly half.

Irv - Ah still wan' to sleep-in.

Irv - *Swanee, how ah lub ya how ah lub ya, ma dear ol' Swanee.*

Roy - Das a song, ain it?

Irv - Yeah!

Roy - How's it go?

Irv - *Ah'd gib da worl' to be, among da folks in D-I-X-I-E eben tho ma mammy's waitin' fo' me, prayin' fo' me down by de Swanee.*

Roy - Wa de *Swanee.*

Irv - De *Swanee's* a ribber down *South.*

Roy - How's it end?

Irv - *De foks up North will see me no more when ah get to dat Swanee shore.*

Roy - He goin' South, ah take it. Hoo wrote dat?

Irv - *Imma notta kno.*

Roy - Ah din tink yu'd kno'. Ahl luk it tup on de

Internet. Here it is. It wer' written in 1919 by George Gershwin wen he wer' 20-years-ol' wile on de bus in Man-hat-tan an' it took him 15 minutes.

Irv - Yu usin' de *Internet* fo' brains, eh?

Roy - De *Internet* shud be part o' *YO* brains.

Irv - Ah hab brains.

Roy - Done soun' lak it.

Irv - Kan yu tell me de *Capital o' Minnesita?*

Roy - *NO!* Yu cain't eider.

Irv - Ah cud use de *Internet* as brains lak yu an' look it tup. It's *Saint Paul* an' *sit-u-a-ted* on high-bluffs ober-lukin de *Mississippi Ribber. North* part, dat is.

Roy - Yu almos' luked lak yu had brains, eben tho, but ah tink ah ben *de-luded.*

Irv - Wa *de-lu-ded?*

Roy - *Decieved in mind an' judge-ment.*

Irv - Ah also knos wa *ha-lluc-i-na-ted* means.

Roy - Ah already knos wa it means. Wa yu tink it means?

Irv - Seein' sump-tin not der.

Roy - Lak wa?

Irv - See a banana, an it luks lak a *Pink-Elephant.*

Roy - *Elephants* ain' *Pink.*

Irv - Das wy it's a *Ha-lluc-i-na-shun.*

Roy - *Dumbo* saw *Pink-Elephants* in de pick-shur called *Dumbo.*

Irv - *How bout Orange-Alli-ga-tors.*

Roy - Der ain' no *Orange-Alli-ga-tors.*

Irv - Das wy it's a *Ha-llu-ci-na-shun.*

Roy - *Sump-times* yu too *smat* fo' me.

Irv - Ah hab ma ways. Now ah wanna sing, *Pink-Elephants* how ah lub ya, how ah lub ya, ma dear ol' *Pink-Elephants.*

Roy - Yu stealin' dat song.

Irv - Ah'd gib da worl' to be among da folks

in *D-U-M-B-O* eben tho da jailors waitin' fo' me, prayin' fo' me down by de *Pink-Elephant*.

Roy - Wa's *Pink-Elephant?*

Irv - *Hallucination!* de folks up *North* will see me no more, wen ah get to dat *Orange-Alligator* shore.

Roy - Hoo wrote dat?

Irv - Ah done it ma-sef. Yu *unner-est-i-mates* me, Ah smat-ter dan yu stink – ah mean yu tink.

Roy - Yu jus' said stink, sted o' tink.

Irv - No-buddy's perfeck.

Roy - Cept me.

Irv - Yu not perfeck, jus' cause yu tink yu are.

Roy - We *boff* smart an' *boff* dumb.

Irv - Take yo choice.

Pole Vaultin' 47

Irv - Ah catch-er by de banana's, swing er ober ma haid an tro her in de pond.

Roy - Hoo yu gonna do dat to?

Irv - Ma girl-fren.

Roy - Wa she do now?

Irv - *She for-got* ma *birf-day.*

Roy - Wen yo *birf-day?*

Irv - A week fum las' *Tuesday.*

Roy - Wa day today?

Irv - Dis *Wed-neds-day.*

Roy - Dat mean yo' birf-day's a week fum las' *Tuesday wich'd be* nex' *Tuesday?*

Irv - Heck! Ah knew dat.

Roy - She thoat yo' *birf-day* wa nex' Tues-day.

Irv - Wa?

Roy - She kno today ib *Wed-nes-day,* an' yo birf-day ib nex' *Tuesday,* so she din *fo-get.*

Irv - Yu *mean ah fo-got?*

Roy - Yu for-got. Yu better *ap-pol-o-gize.*

Irv - Den ah gess ah better *NOT swing er ober ma haid an'* tro her in de pond.

Roy - Now yu' is cookin' wif tomato sauce, es-spec-cially if she gonna gib yu a *birf-day* present.

Irv - Ah asss-ed fo' a *pro-fess-shun-al* pole fo' ma hobby o' *pole-vaultin'.*

Roy - Yu tink she'd gib yu dat?

Irv - She kno's how ah lak to take de bamboo *clothes-line* pole, an' run up-an-down de yard an' vault ober de *clothes-line.*

Roy - Yu doan need no bran new pole to jump ober no *clothes-line.* Yu all-reddy gotta pole.

Irv - Ah needs one o' dose *profess-shun-al* ultra-bendy ones to vault in de air, an' de pole bends double, den snap's yu high in de air an' ober de *clothes-line.*

Roy - Aren't yu afraid yore feet mite catch in de

clothes-line an' yu go *rumblin'-tumblin'* down to lan' face-down in a big *mud-puddle?*

Irv - Schn-snot rainin'.

Roy - Yu in sum kinda *compe-ti-shun,* or wa?

Irv - Ah gonna go for a win at de *Olympics.*

Roy – Fo dat yu need a coach or sump-tin.

Irv - Ah cud get de hi-school coach if he wa *sober* enuff.

Roy - De coach hab a dinkin' problem?

Irv - He wishes he dint, but cain't hep his-sef.

Roy - Dat bad. eh?

Irv - Cummin' home fum a track meet his car wen off de road, down de hill an' into de surf wer it came to a stop, hit by waves wif horn a-blowin'.

Roy - May-be yore mud-der an' fad-der cud hep yu pay fo' a more *re-ly-able* coach.

Irv - Some doan lak pole-vaultin' cause dey fraid ah mite use it fo' ma own gain.

Roy - How dat?

    Irv - Wif ma own pole-vault pole ah mite run at de clear-glass o' a jewel-ry store, bash in de glass, an' tro a pile o' jewel-ry in de wagon an' take off.

Roy - Dat soun' far-fetched.

    Irv - Specially since ah doan lak *jewel-ry* any-way. Tho ah *sup-pose* ah cud gib sum *jewel-ry* to ma girl-fren.

Roy - Wud she tank yu?

    Irv - She'd prob-ley ask wer'd yu get dis *jewel-ry,* an' ah'd hab to say, ah took de *pole-vault pole,* knock-ed a hole in de *jewel-ry* store glass an' stole yu de *jewel-ry.*

Roy - Das honest ob yu, but stupid ob yu. Wa wud she say?

    Irv - Prob-ley *tank yu berry much.*

Roy - *We're Off to see de Wizard, de Woner-full Wizard o' Oz.*

Irv - Wy we *Off to see de Wizard, de Woner-full Wizard o' Oz?*

Roy - Cause da's *Imagination.*

Irv - Wa ib *imag-i-na-shun?*

Roy - *Imagination* ib formin' images in de mine dat's not really der.

Irv - Wa?

Roy - Lak ah seeeee in maaaaa mine's a *pick-ture* o' *Inky-Pinky-Ombli-Goo.*

Irv - Wa do he luk lak?

Roy - He sorta luk's lak a *Gob-lin.*

Irv - Ah doan kno' wa no *Gob-lin* luk lak.

Roy - Do ah gotta draw yu a *pick-shur,* or wa?

Irv - Yeah! Draw me a *pick-shur.*

Roy - Dis a book, it doan hab no *pick-shurs*.

   Irv - Den how ah goin' to kno' wa a *Inky-Pinky-Ombli-Goo* luk lak?

Roy - Ah doan hab no time to draw yu no *pick-shur* o' no *Inky-Pinky-Ombli-Goo* innna book dats 'bout sump-tin else.

   Irv - Den wy'd yu bring-up sump-tin lak *Inky-Pinky-Ombli-Goo* dat re-quire *pick-shurs?*

Roy - Yu can also tell *imagination* by usin' WORDS.

   Irv - Wa?

Roy - WORDS in *imagination* is we're *Off to see de Wizard, de Woner-Full Wizard o' Oz.*

   Irv - Wy din yu say so?

Roy - Der ain' no *real* fab-u-lous *Wizard* an' der ain' no city o' *Oz* cause it's *imag-in-a-shun'* in WORDS.

   Irv - Well, by ma *Honkey-Donk!*

Roy - No! Das wa *im-ag-i-na-shun is.* It's also called *cre-a-ti-vi-ti-diddy.*

   Irv - Sort o' a big lie, eh?

Roy - *WORDS* is sort-o' a big lie, but if yu lie often enuff, it look lak yu tellin' de *TROOFF.*

Irv - Yu mean *imag-i-na-shun* ib sort o' tellin' de *TROOFF wich ib not de TROOFF?*

Roy - It wer made-dup by L. Frank Baum in 1900. He died at 63-years ol'.

Irv - Any-buddy else in dat *imag-i-na-shun story?*

Roy - In de story, der wer' characters lak *Dorothy,* de' teen-age daugh-ter hoo went bonkers wile in de house wen it wer blown high ober de prairies by a *hurr-i-kane.*

Irv - Dat soun' stupid.

Roy - Der wer' Toto, *Dorothy's* dog, de *Scarecrow,* de *Tin Woodman,* de *Cowardly Lion,* an' ob-corse, de *Wizard o' Oz.*

Irv - Hoo else wer der?

Roy - Der wer' de *Good Wich,* de *Wicked Wich o' de West,* de *Yel-low Brick Road,* an' *Emeral City-bunky.*

Irv - In de end, did dey cum out o' it, OK?

Roy - Yep! Dey cum outo it OK. Wa yu re-spect, a *UN-*happy ending?

Irv - Ah thoat dey wud in-heret a buncha money an' fly to *Alaska.*

Roy - Wy dey gonna do dat? It too cole in *Alaska.* Wen it snows yu cain't eben see nuffin.

Irv - Well, den fly to de *Amazon Ribber* an' go *cannoo-in' in de rain.*

Roy - Yu ain gonna do dat, but yu *IS* usin' yo own *imag-i-na-shun.*

Irv - Ah hab *img-i-na-shun?*

Roy - Yu jus' re-Xpressed yore-sef in *imag-i-na-shun.*

Irv - Do ah git a medal?

Roy - Nope.

Empire State Buildin' 49

Roy - Wa ya goin' ta do ta-day, Irv?

Irv - Gonna see *Fred,* it-needs to be said, he's not been fed, he ain' dead, an' needs a bed.

Roy - Yu doan hab to see no *Fred.* Ah kno' him, he ridin' de *merry-go-roun'* at *Bumboldt Bark,* ah mean *Humboldt Park.*

Irv - Ah laks *crazy-ness* in ma life.

Roy - Wa 'bout jumpin' off de roof o' de *Empire State Buildin'?*

Irv - How hi dat buildin'?

Roy - *Internet* say de *Empire State Buildin'* ib *1250* feet high an' de *an-tenn-a* reach *1454* feet high.

Irv - No shit!

Roy - It be de *43rd* talles' buildin' in de worl', or my name ain' *Dolly Parton.*

Irv - *1250* feet ib taller dan ma *Uncle Harry.*

Roy - How tall he?

Irv - On a dry day, he *seben-foot-eleben*, an' countin'.

Roy - Wooo-eee! Dat higher dan a kite loose in a *hurri-kane*.

Irv - Waaaba yuuuba goin' ta do today, Roy?

Roy - Ah asss-ed yu firs'.

Irv - Ah gonna wake up in da mornin', wif ma haid held high, an' gaze into de mornin' wif jus' a liddle sigh.

Roy - Ah kin see, yu doan kno' eider.

Irv - Ah repeats, waaaba yuuuba goin' to do today, Roy?

Roy - Ah gonna be free, cause ah'm a liddle *HE*, wer' nailed to a tree, ah foun' a liddle key, allowin' such as me to sip a bit o' tea an' make a liddle pee.

Irv - Sayin' pea is *un-kuth!*

Roy - Ah din claim ah was *kuth.*

Irv - Yu wer' *un-kuth!*

Roy - Yu doan eben kno' how to spell *kuth*, or *un-kuth*. Act-ually, neider do ah.

Irv - Ah ain' no *lit-er-ary* genius.

Roy – Das fo' sure!

Irv - Yu ain no *lit-er-rary* genius eider.

Roy - Wa ib ah den?

Irv - Yu a *cucumber* bent double in da middle color-ed *orange*.

Roy - Das quite *imag-i-na-tive*. Yu eber tink o' bein' a artist?

Irv - Ah thunk 'bout it once.

Roy - How cum yu let it slip thru yo fingers, or lak droppin' a jelly-dish on de floor, or yankin' de stick bak wile pullin' out o' a nose-dive to avoid crash-in' into a mountain-side?

Irv - Usin' all dem *de-scrip-shuns,* ain yu bein' a liddel *melo-dram-a-tic?*

Roy - Jus' speakin' de truth wif a capital *"T".*

Irv - Ah goin' down to de warf an' catch some *bigguns.*

Roy – Wa, *big mosquito bites?*

Irv - No! Big *fish.*

Roy - Yu gotta *fishin' pole?*

  Irv - Nope!

Roy - Yu got-*ainy bate?*

  Irv - Nope!

Roy - Yu cain't go fishin' if yu doan hab no *re-quip-ment.*

  Irv - Den ahl go *swimmin'.*

Roy - Yu kno' how to *swim?*

  Irv - *Nope!*

Roy - Yu a movin' accident goin' sum-place to happen.

  Irv - Ah cud eat a *burger.*

Roy - Wa kine o' *burger?*

  Irv - Wif *lettuce, tomato, onions, may-yo-nayse an' ket-tchup.*

Roy - Yu got de *money?*

  Irv - Nope!

Down in de Balley 50

Roy - *Down in de balley, balley so lo.*
Hang yore haid ober. Hear de win blo.
Hang yore head ober, hear de win blo.
Hang yore haid ober, hear de win blo.

Irv - Wy ma spossed to do dat?

Roy - Cause yu a nin-com-poop an' doan kno' no better.

Irv - Ah is not!

Roy - *Roses lub Sun-shine, Violets lub Dew.*
Angels in Heben kno' ah lub yu.
Kno' ah lub yu dear, kno' ah lub yu.
Angels in Heben kno' ah lub yu.

Irv - Ah want-ta say ma piece.

Roy - Shut up an' sit down.
If yu doan lub me, lub whom yu please.
Tro yore arms roun' me gib ma hart ease.
Giv ma hart ease, lub, gib ma hart ease.
Tro yore arms roun' me, gib ma hart ease.

Irv - *Blah! Blah! Blah!*

Roy - Build me a castle forty feet high.
        So Ah kin see him as he rides by.
        As he rides by, lub, as he rides by,
        So ah can see him, as he rides by.

  Irv - Ah gonna keep squakin' til ah say ma piece!

Roy - Wha-ever.
        Write me a led-der send it by mail
        Send it in care o' Birmingham Jail
        Birmingham Jail, lub, Birmingham Jail.
        Send it in care of Birmingham Jail.

  Irv - *Yubba Yubba Yubba, Ugga Boo Boo Ugga.*

Roy - Da's sayin' yo piece? Da's no piece. Yu cudda
        waited.

  Irv - Ah felt ignored. Wy yu sing *Down in de Balley*
        in de firs' place?

Roy - Cause it meaning-ful to me. He a cuntry-boy
        libbin out in de fields, but un-happy cause he in
        lub wif his *girl-fren* an' done sump-tin rong.

  Irv - How yu kno' dat?

Roy - Cause he hangin' his haid lo-down an' hearin' de
        win' blo.

  Irv - May-be dey's a storm shuutin down de path
        an' waitin' to drown de *be-jesus* out o' em.

Roy - Doan yu hab no poetic juices in yo blud?

Irv - Ah had orange-juice fo' break-fas'.

Roy - Yu jus' proo-ved ma point.

Irv - Ah laks it wif toast an jelly.

Roy - Den he links his-sef wif sun-shine, violets, dew an lub fo' his *girl-fren* wif angels in *Heben*.

Irv - Dat does kinda drop da final nail in de coffin an' slammin' it shut fo' de etern-i-diddy o' life.

Roy - Den he *re-magines* his girl-fren tro-in her arms roun' him, an' gibbin him a big squeeze fum da bottom-up o' her lub an' ex-pressin' da carrin' his *mud-der* wa spossed to gib him, but din't.

Irv - How yu kno' hib mud-der din gib him no lub?

Roy - Patience my dear boy an' yu'll fine out. He then want a castle, 40-feet-high so he can see *God* as he rides by an' *God* can see him as a *re-sample* o' *God's* guuud work an' dey can *re-preciate* each odder'.

Irv - Wow! Ah din' kno' der wer' dat much in de song.

Roy - Yu hab been *ed-u-kate-ted* an' now kno's de ultimate secret o' *God* an' mankind.

Irv - Wa dat, *Massa?*

Roy - Yu fine out in de las' *para-grafff!*

Irv - Wa dat?

Roy - We fine out he in de *Birmingham Jail* fo' a krime we hope he din commit, but probably did.

Irv - Wa he do?

Roy - He doan tell us dat story. Probably robbed a bunk, ah mean bank, or ticked off de high-school principal, or ran a red-light. Do dat teach yu a lesson?

Irv - Yep! It do.

Roy - Wa it teach yu?

Irv - Luk boff ways befo' crossin de street.

Other Books by Doug Rucker

Personal Journey
  Poems predicting next phase of life.

Early Stories
  Autobiography Birth - University.

Groundwork
  Autobiography - Marriage & office.

Growing Edge
  Autobiography – Office & Recreation.

Moving Through
  Poems & "No Think" pastels.

Book of Words
  Short Stories - Humor & philosophy.

Harold & the Acid Sea of Reality
  Thoughts on fantasy & reality.

Trial by Fire
  Burning & rebuilding personal home.

Building a Home that Loves You
  Architectural Philosophy - pictures.

Transitions
  Realism, Reflections & Abstract.

Thinking in the Abstract
  Deciphering abstract art.

Poetries
  Poems - Abstract Art/ Poetry.

Brief Biography

Born on the last day of 1927, and after finishing eigth grade in Lombard, Illinois, Doug was awarded a scholarship to the Chicago Art Institute before entering Austin High School, in Chicago. In sports, football, swimming and track he was awarded 7 letters while pursuing a 3 - year course in architecture. At the University of Illlinois between 1945 and 1950, he completed his Bachelor of Science degree and thereafter worked as a draftsman in Denver, San Diego and Pasadena. There, he married his first wife, Karon and soon after became a licensed architect and had 3 marvelous daughters. While working as an important designer/draftsman in a Brentwood Village architectural firm, he designed and built their first house his family lived in for about 5 years. In 1966 he built another Malibu dream house, a *"House of the Heart"*, the main floor floating on a 26-foot square pedestal, 40-feet high in the air with wrap-around decks and spectacular views of the ocean, shore line and Surfrider's Beach. He received much newspaper and magazine notoriety before it was burned to the ground in 1970 by a devastating brush fire. By 1972 he'd built another more fire-resistant *"House of the Head"* over the same foundations. It can be found in the, Architectural Guidebook to Los Angeles by David Gebhard and Robert Winter. It was similarly honored, but lost to a divorce in 1980. His new wife, Marge, and he enjoyed 36 years of creative life in a very small house he designed on an acre of land in the mountains above Point Dume in the County of Los Angeles. Marge died of various illnesses in December, 2016. Now retired at the age of 97, Doug lives alone cared for by his three daughters, Viveka, Lilianne and Amanda, son-in-law Tom Rincker, and Minerva his part-time caretaker and her dog.

www.ingramcontent.com/pod-product-compliance
Lightning Source LLC
Chambersburg PA
CBHW041934260326
41914CB00010B/1293